FAVORITE BRAND NAME
PASTA

Publications International, Ltd.

Pictured on the front cover: Pasta e Fagioli *(page 12)*.

ISBN: 0-7853-2451-8

Manufactured in U.S.A.

8 7 6 5 4 3 2 1

Nutritional Analysis: Nutritional information is given for some of the
recipes in this publication. Each analysis is based on the food items in
the ingredient list, except ingredients labeled as "optional" or "for
garnish." When more than one ingredient choice is listed, the first
ingredient is used for analysis. If a range for the amount of an
ingredient is given, the nutritional analysis is based on the lowest
amount. Foods offered as "serve with" suggestions are not included in
the analysis unless otherwise stated.

Microwave Cooking: Microwave ovens vary in wattage. Use the cooking
times as guidelines and check for doneness before adding more time.

FAVORITE BRAND NAME
PASTA

Savory
SOUPS &
SALADS

Quick Beef Soup

1½ pounds lean ground beef
1 cup chopped onion
2 cloves garlic, finely chopped
1 can (28 ounces) tomatoes, undrained
6 cups water
6 beef bouillon cubes
¼ teaspoon black pepper
½ cup uncooked orzo
1½ cups frozen peas, carrots and corn
    vegetable blend
French bread (optional)

Cook beef, onion and garlic in large saucepan over medium-high heat until beef is brown, stirring to separate meat; drain fat.

Process tomatoes with juice in blender or food processor until smooth. Add tomatoes, water, bouillon cubes and pepper to meat mixture. Bring to a boil; reduce heat to low. Simmer, uncovered, 20 minutes. Add orzo and vegetables. Simmer an additional 15 minutes. Serve with French bread, if desired.

Makes 6 servings

Favorite recipe from **North Dakota Beef Commission**

Sausage Minestrone Soup

2 tablespoons olive oil
1 large onion, chopped
3 cloves garlic, minced
3 cups water
1 can (14½ ounces) stewed tomatoes, undrained
1 can (10½ ounces) kosher condensed beef or chicken broth
1 teaspoon dried basil leaves
1 teaspoon dried oregano leaves
¼ teaspoon crushed red pepper
1 package (12 ounces) HEBREW NATIONAL® Lean Smoked Turkey Sausage
½ cup small pasta such as ditalini or small bow ties
1 can (16 ounces) cannellini beans, drained

Heat oil in large saucepan over medium heat. Add onion and garlic; cook 8 minutes, stirring occasionally. Add water, tomatoes with liquid, broth, basil, oregano and crushed pepper; bring to a boil.

Meanwhile, cut sausage crosswise into ½-inch slices. Cut each slice into quarters. Stir sausage and pasta into soup; simmer 15 minutes or until pasta is tender. Add beans; cook until heated through.

Makes 6 servings

Tortellini Soup

1 tablespoon margarine
2 cloves garlic, minced
2 cans (13¾ fluid ounces each)
    COLLEGE INN® Chicken or Beef
    Broth
1 package (8 ounces) fresh or frozen
    cheese-filled tortellini, thawed
1 can (14½ ounces) stewed tomatoes, cut
    up, undrained
1 package (10 ounces) fresh or frozen
    spinach, thawed
   Grated Parmesan cheese

In large saucepan, melt margarine over medium-high heat. Add garlic; cook and stir 2 to 3 minutes or until lightly browned. Add broth and tortellini; bring to a boil. Reduce heat to low; simmer 10 minutes, stirring occasionally. Add tomatoes and spinach; simmer an additional 5 minutes. Top individual servings with Parmesan cheese.   *Makes 6 servings*

Super Simple Chicken Soup

- 4 cups water
- 1 can (14½ ounces) chicken broth
- 2 teaspoons soy sauce
- 3 boned and skinned chicken breast halves
- 1⅓ cups SONOMA® Dried Tomato Halves, snipped into quarters
- ½ cup uncooked elbow macaroni
- ⅓ cup sliced green onions
- ½ teaspoon dried thyme leaves
- 1 package (10 ounces) frozen peas and carrots

In 3-quart saucepan combine water, broth and soy sauce; bring to boil. Cut chicken into 1-inch chunks and add to liquid with tomatoes. Simmer 10 minutes. Add macaroni, onions and thyme. Simmer until macaroni is cooked, about 10 minutes, adding peas and carrots after 5 minutes.

Makes 4 to 6 main-dish servings (about 2 quarts)

Ravioli Soup

8 ounces sweet Italian sausage, casing removed
1 clove garlic, crushed
2 (13¾-fluid ounce) cans COLLEGE INN® Lower Sodium Chicken Broth
2 cups water
1 (9-ounce) package frozen miniature cheese-filled ravioli
1 (15-ounce) can garbanzo beans, drained
1 (14½-ounce) can stewed tomatoes
⅓ cup GREY POUPON® Dijon Mustard
½ teaspoon dried oregano leaves
¼ teaspoon coarsely ground black pepper
1 cup torn fresh spinach leaves
Grated Parmesan cheese

In 4-quart heavy pot, over medium heat, brown sausage and cook garlic until tender, stirring to break up sausage, about 5 minutes. Pour off excess fat; remove sausage mixture from pot and set aside.

In same pot, over medium-high heat, heat chicken broth and water to a boil. Add ravioli; cook for 4 to 5 minutes or until tender. Stir in beans, stewed tomatoes, sausage mixture, mustard, oregano and pepper; heat through. Stir in spinach and cook until wilted, about 1 minute. Serve topped with Parmesan cheese. *Makes 8 servings*

Chicken Noodle & Vegetable Soup

  2   tablespoons margarine or butter
  ¾   pound skinless, boneless chicken
        breasts or thighs, cut into ½-inch
        pieces
  1   cup chopped onion
  2   cups frozen mixed broccoli, cauliflower
        and carrots vegetable medley
  1   can (13¾ ounces) reduced-sodium or
        regular chicken broth
  ¼   teaspoon dried thyme leaves or dried
        basil
  ⅛   teaspoon black pepper
  1   package (4.7 ounces) PASTA RONI®
        Chicken Broccoli with Linguine

1. In 3-quart saucepan, melt margarine over medium heat. Add chicken and onion; cook, stirring occasionally, 4 to 5 minutes or until chicken is no longer pink.

2. Add 1½ cups water, frozen vegetables, chicken broth and seasonings. Bring just to a boil.

3. Gradually add pasta while stirring. Separate pasta with a fork, if needed.

4. Stir in contents of seasoning packet.

5. Boil, uncovered, stirring frequently, 9 to 10 minutes or until pasta is desired tenderness.   *4 servings*

Alphabet Turkey Soup

4 cups turkey broth or reduced-sodium
    chicken bouillon
1 can (16 ounces) tomatoes, undrained
1 cup chopped onion
1 cup thinly sliced carrots
2 teaspoons dried Italian seasoning
½ teaspoon salt
¼ teaspoon pepper
4 cups thinly sliced cabbage
2 cups (½-inch) cubed cooked turkey
½ cup alphabet pasta

1. In 5-quart saucepan over medium-high heat, combine broth, tomatoes, onion, carrots, Italian seasoning, salt and pepper; bring to a boil. Reduce to low; simmer 10 to 15 minutes or until carrots are tender.

2. Add cabbage, turkey and pasta; return to a boil. Cook 5 to 10 minutes or until cabbage and pasta are tender.

Makes 8 servings

Favorite recipe from **National Turkey Federation**

Pasta e Fagioli

2 tablespoons olive oil
1 cup chopped onion
3 cloves garlic, minced
2 cans (14½ ounces each) Italian-style
   stewed tomatoes, undrained
3 cups ⅓-less-salt chicken broth
1 can (about 15 ounces) cannellini beans
   (white kidney beans), undrained*
¼ cup chopped fresh Italian parsley
1 teaspoon dried basil leaves
¼ teaspoon ground black pepper
4 ounces uncooked small shell pasta

1. Heat oil in 4-quart Dutch oven over medium heat until hot; add onion and garlic. Cook and stir 5 minutes or until onion is tender.

2. Stir tomatoes with liquid, chicken broth, beans with liquid, parsley, basil and pepper into Dutch oven; bring to a boil over high heat, stirring occasionally. Reduce heat to low. Simmer, covered, 10 minutes.

3. Add pasta to Dutch oven. Simmer, covered, 10 to 12 minutes or until pasta is just tender. Serve immediately. Garnish as desired.

Makes 8 servings

*One can (about 15 ounces) Great Northern beans, undrained, may be substituted for cannellini beans.

White Cheddar Seafood Chowder

    2   tablespoons margarine or butter
    ½   cup chopped onion
  2¼   cups water
    1   package (6.2 ounces) PASTA RONI®
          Shells & White Cheddar
    1   cup sliced carrots
    ½   teaspoon salt (optional)
    ¾   pound fresh or thawed frozen firm
          white fish, cut into ½-inch pieces
  1¼   cups milk
    2   tablespoons chopped parsley (optional)

1. In 3-quart saucepan, melt margarine over medium heat. Add onion; saute 1 minute.

2. Add water; bring to a boil over high heat.

3. Stir in pasta, carrots and salt.

4. Bring just to a boil. Reduce heat to medium. Boil, uncovered, stirring frequently, 12 minutes.

5. Add fish, milk, parsley and contents of seasoning packet. Continue cooking 3 to 4 minutes, stirring occasionally, or until pasta is desired tenderness and fish is opaque.   *Makes 4 servings*

Hearty Fettuccine, Ham and Bean Soup

2 tablespoons olive oil
1 cup canned chunky Italian tomato
   sauce
2 cloves garlic, chopped
1 cup diced cooked ham
4 cups canned no-fat, low-salt chicken
   broth, divided
1 (15-ounce) can garbanzo beans,
   drained, divided
4 ounces fettuccine (broken into thirds),
   elbows or rotini
   Parmesan cheese

Heat oil in saucepan over medium heat. Add tomato
sauce, garlic and ham. Simmer 5 minutes. Add 3 cups
broth; stir to blend. Purée remaining broth and 1 cup
garbanzo beans in blender. Add to saucepan; add
remaining garbanzo beans. Bring to a boil, reduce heat
and simmer 10 minutes. Add pasta; cook until tender,
about 10 minutes. Serve, passing Parmesan cheese
separately.   *Makes 4 to 6 servings*

Favorite recipe from **North Dakota Wheat Commission**

Creamy Minestrone Soup

1 package (5.1 ounces) PASTA RONI®
  Angel Hair Pasta with Parmesan
  Cheese
1 can (15 ounces) kidney beans, rinsed,
  drained
1 can (15 or 16 ounces) cannellini or
  Great Northern beans, rinsed, drained
1 can (14½ ounces) tomatoes, undrained,
  chopped
1 can (13¾ ounces) reduced-sodium or
  regular chicken broth
1 large zucchini, chopped
1 teaspoon dried basil
1 teaspoon dried marjoram leaves or dried
  oregano leaves
2 tablespoons grated Parmesan cheese
  (optional)
2 tablespoons chopped Italian parsley or
  parsley (optional)

1. In 3-quart saucepan, combine pasta, contents of
seasoning packet, 2 cups water, beans, tomatoes,
chicken broth, zucchini and seasonings. Bring just to a
boil. Separate pasta with a fork, if needed. Reduce heat
to medium.

2. Simmer, stirring occasionally, 7 to 8 minutes or
until pasta and zucchini are tender. Additional water
may be added if soup thickens.

3. Ladle into soup bowls. Sprinkle with cheese and
parsley, if desired.   *5 servings*

Colorful Grape, Pepper and Pasta Salad

8 ounces dry thin spaghetti, cooked
  Mustard Vinaigrette (recipe follows)
1 cup California seedless grapes
½ cup thinly sliced red or yellow bell
  pepper
2 tablespoons minced celery
2 tablespoons green onion
1 tablespoon chopped fresh tarragon*
  Salt and pepper to taste
¼ cup walnuts, quartered**
  Fresh tarragon sprigs (optional)

Combine cooked spaghetti and 3 tablespoons Mustard
Vinaigrette; toss to coat and cool. Add remaining
ingredients including vinaigrette; mix well. Serve in
lettuce-lined bowl; garnish with tarragon sprigs, if
desired.   *Makes 4 servings*

*One-half teaspoon dried tarragon, crushed, may be substituted.

**Walnuts may be omitted; substitute 1 tablespoon walnut oil for 1
tablespoon olive oil in vinaigrette.

Mustard Vinaigrette: Combine 3 tablespoons white
wine vinegar, 2 tablespoons olive oil, 2 tablespoons
Dijon mustard, 1 clove minced garlic, ½ teaspoon sugar
and ⅛ teaspoon pepper; mix well.

Makes about ⅓ cup

Favorite recipe from **California Table Grape Commission**

Pasta and Walnut Fruit Salad

½ (1-pound) package of medium pasta
    shells, uncooked
1 (8-ounce) container of nonfat plain
    yogurt
¼ cup frozen orange juice concentrate,
    thawed
1 (15-ounce) can juice-pack mandarin
    oranges, drained
1 cup seedless red grapes, cut into halves
1 cup seedless green grapes, cut into
    halves
1 apple, cored and chopped
½ cup sliced celery
½ cup walnut halves

Cook shells according to package directions; drain. In
small bowl, blend yogurt and orange juice concentrate.
In large bowl, combine shells and remaining
ingredients. Add yogurt mixture; toss to coat. Cover;
chill thoroughly.   *Makes 6 to 8 servings*

Pasta Substitutions: mostaccioli, elbow macaroni,
rotini, farfalle.

Favorite recipe from **Walnut Marketing Board**

Caribbean Pasta Salad with Tropical Island Dressing

1   can black beans, drained and rinsed
½   cup thawed orange juice concentrate
½   teaspoon ground allspice
6   ounces mafalda pasta
1   teaspoon vegetable oil
4   cups washed and torn romaine lettuce
    leaves
1½ cups fresh pineapple chunks
1   mango, peeled and sliced
1   cup shredded cabbage
⅓   cup chopped onion
⅓   cup chopped red bell pepper
8   ounces piña colada-flavored yogurt
½   cup orange juice
1   teaspoon grated fresh ginger
2   oranges

1. Combine beans, juice concentrate and allspice in medium bowl. Cover and refrigerate 1 hour; drain and discard liquid from beans.

2. Cook pasta according to package directions. Drain. Rinse under cold water until cool; drain again. Return to pan; toss with oil.

3. To assemble salad, divide lettuce, pasta, pineapple, beans, mango, cabbage, onion and bell pepper among 6 plates.

4. To prepare dressing, combine yogurt, orange juice and ginger in small bowl. Remove colored portion of peel of 1 orange using vegetable peeler. Finely chop peel to measure 1 tablespoon; stir into dressing. Remove white portion of peel from orange and peel remaining orange. Separate oranges into sections; arrange on salads. Serve with dressing.

Makes 6 servings

Italian Rotini Salad

1 **(12-ounce) package tricolor rotini pasta, cooked, drained**
1 **pound cooked roast beef, cut into ½-inch cubes (about 2 cups)**
2 **cups broccoli flowerettes, blanched**
4 **ounces provolone cheese, cut into ¼-inch cubes (about 1 cup)**
⅓ **cup purchased roasted red peppers, coarsely chopped**
¾ **cup A.1.® ORIGINAL or A.1.® BOLD Steak Sauce**
½ **cup purchased Italian dressing**

In large nonmetallic bowl, combine pasta, beef, broccoli, cheese and peppers. In small bowl, blend steak sauce and dressing; pour over pasta mixture, tossing to coat well. Refrigerate at least 1 hour before serving.

Makes 8 servings

Warm Pasta and Spinach Salad

1   package (10 ounces) fresh spinach,
        washed, stems removed and torn into
        bite-size pieces
½   pound mushrooms, sliced
8   ounces MUELLER'S® Ziti or Twists
        (3 or 4 cups), cooked, rinsed with
        cold water and drained
1   medium red onion, sliced
6   slices uncooked bacon, coarsely
        chopped
1   tablespoon ARGO® or KINGSFORD'S®
        Corn Starch
1   tablespoon sugar
1   teaspoon salt
½   teaspoon pepper
1   cup HELLMANN'S® or BEST FOODS®
        Real or Low Fat Mayonnaise Dressing
1   cup water
⅓   cup cider vinegar

1. In large serving bowl, toss spinach, mushrooms,
pasta and red onion; set aside.

2. In medium skillet, cook bacon over medium-high
heat until crisp. Remove with slotted spoon. Pour off
all but 2 tablespoons drippings.

3. In small bowl, mix corn starch, sugar, salt and
pepper. With wire whisk, stir corn starch mixture into
drippings in skillet until smooth. Blend in mayonnaise.

Gradually stir in water and vinegar. Over medium heat, bring mixture to a boil; boil 1 minute.

4. Pour over spinach mixture. Add bacon; toss to coat well. Serve immediately.   *Makes 8 to 10 servings*

Greek Pasta Salad

½ **pound extra-lean (90% lean) ground beef**
⅓ **cup chopped fresh mint *or* 2 tablespoons dried leaf mint**
1 **garlic clove, minced**
1¾ **cups (about 6 ounces) small shell macaroni, cooked**
10 **cherry tomatoes, quartered**
2 **ounces feta cheese, crumbled**
½ **red bell pepper, chopped**
½ **red onion, cut into rings**
¼ **cup reduced-calorie Italian dressing**
2 **tablespoons lemon juice**
   Salt and freshly ground black pepper
   Lettuce leaves

Brown ground beef in medium skillet. Drain. Add mint and garlic; cook 2 minutes, stirring constantly.

Spoon ground beef mixture into large bowl. Stir in pasta, tomatoes, cheese, red bell pepper and onion. Add dressing and lemon juice; toss lightly. Season with salt and black pepper to taste. Serve on lettuce-covered salad plates.   *Makes 4 servings*

Note: Salad can be made up to 4 hours in advance.

Cajun Pork with Pasta Salad

1 boneless pork tenderloin (about
    12 ounces), visible fat trimmed
    Cajun Spice Rub (page 23)
    Nonstick cooking spray
8 ounces fresh or frozen, thawed sliced
    okra
½ red bell pepper, sliced
½ yellow bell pepper, sliced
1 teaspoon minced jalapeño pepper
1 small onion, sliced
¼ cup fat-free reduced-sodium chicken
    broth
8 ounces farfalle pasta, cooked and kept
    warm

1. Cut pork into ¼-inch-thick slices; coat with Cajun Spice Rub. Spray skillet with cooking spray. Heat over medium heat until hot. Cook and stir pork 2 to 3 minutes on each side until browned. Remove from skillet.

2. Add okra to skillet; cook 3 to 5 minutes or until browned. Add bell peppers, jalapeño pepper, onion and chicken broth; bring to a boil. Reduce heat; simmer, covered, 3 to 5 minutes or until vegetables are crisp-tender. Add pork and cook 2 to 3 minutes. Season to taste with salt and black pepper. Place pasta on platter; spoon pork mixture over top and toss.

Makes 4 main-dish servings

Cajun Spice Rub

2 teaspoons dried oregano leaves
1 teaspoon garlic powder
1 teaspoon dried thyme leaves
½ teaspoon dried mustard
½ teaspoon paprika
¼ teaspoon salt
¼ teaspoon dried cumin
¼ teaspoon ground allspice
¼ teaspoon ground red pepper
¼ teaspoon black pepper

1. Combine ingredients in small bowl.

Makes about 2 tablespoons

Ranch Italian Pasta Salad

1 pound fusilli or other spiral or shell-
   shaped pasta, cooked and drained
2 cups sliced fresh mushrooms
1½ cups cooked broccoli flowerets
1 cup prepared HIDDEN VALLEY
   RANCH® Ranch Italian salad dressing
4 ounces salami, cut into julienne strips
1 red bell pepper, minced
¼ cup grated Parmesan cheese
2 tablespoons chopped parsley

In large bowl, combine all ingredients, tossing
thoroughly with salad dressing. Cover and refrigerate
at least 1 hour before serving.   *Serves 4 to 6*

Antipasto Salad

1 cup MIRACLE WHIP® Salad Dressing

½ cup milk

2 (0.6-ounce) packages GOOD SEASONS® Zesty Italian Salad Dressing Mix

5⅓ cups (16 ounces) uncooked mostaccioli, cooked and drained

1 (8-ounce) package cotto salami slices, cut into strips

1 (8-ounce) package CASINO® Natural Low-Moisture Part-Skim Mozzarella Cheese, cubed

¾ cup *each* thin red bell pepper strips and thin zucchini strips

½ cup pitted ripe olives, drained, halved

• Mix together salad dressing, milk, dressing mix and pasta in large shallow bowl.

• Arrange remaining ingredients over pasta mixture; cover and chill.

Makes 18 servings (about 14 cups)

Note: Recipe may be cut in half.

Spam™ Mexican Extravaganza

1   cup uncooked tricolor rotini
1   (12-ounce) can SPAM® Luncheon Meat, cubed
1   (15-ounce) can pinto beans, drained
1   cup frozen whole kernel corn, thawed
¾   cup (3 ounces) shredded Cheddar cheese
1   green bell pepper, chopped
¼   cup chopped onion
¼   cup chopped tomato
1   (2¼-ounce) can sliced ripe olives, drained
1   (8-ounce) jar CHI-CHI'S® Salsa
¾   cup sour cream
1   tablespoon mayonnaise or salad dressing
4   cups shredded lettuce
    CHI-CHI'S® Tortilla Chips

Cook rotini according to package directions; drain and refrigerate. In large skillet over medium heat, sauté Spam® until lightly browned; cool. In large bowl, combine rotini, Spam®, beans, corn, cheese, bell pepper, onion, tomato and olives. In small bowl, combine salsa, sour cream and mayonnaise. Toss together salsa mixture and Spam™ mixture. Cover and refrigerate several hours. Spoon salad mixture over lettuce. Serve with chips.   *Makes 6 to 8 servings*

Pasta Chicken Breast Salad

8 ounces rotelle pasta
2 (3-ounce) chicken breasts
2 teaspoons lemon pepper
½ head lettuce
5 fresh spinach leaves
½ cup halved red grapes
½ cup halved strawberries*
Fat-free raspberry vinaigrette dressing

Cook pasta as directed on package. Drain and rinse with cold water; set aside. Sprinkle chicken breasts with lemon pepper and broil or grill over medium heat for 10 minutes, turning once. While pasta and chicken cook, prepare fruit and vegetables. Tear lettuce and spinach; place on 2 dinner plates. Sprinkle pasta, grapes and strawberries over greens. Slice chicken breasts lengthwise and place on top. Serve with vinaigrette dressing.   *Makes 2 servings*

*Seasonal fruit may be substituted

Favorite recipe from **North Dakota Wheat Commission**

Dijon Asparagus Chicken Salad

1 **cup HELLMANN'S® or BEST FOODS®
   Real or Low Fat Mayonnaise Dressing**
¼ **cup HELLMANN'S® or BEST FOODS®
   DIJONNAISE Creamy Mustard Blend**
2 **tablespoons lemon juice**
1 **teaspoon salt**
½ **teaspoon black pepper**
6 **ounces MUELLER'S® Twist Trio®
   (about 2½ cups), cooked and drained**
1 **pound skinless boneless chicken
   breasts, cooked and chopped**
1 **package (10 ounces) frozen asparagus
   spears, thawed and cut into 2-inch
   pieces**
1 **red pepper, cut into 1-inch pieces**

1. In large bowl, combine mayonnaise, creamy mustard blend, lemon juice, salt and black pepper; mix well.

2. Add remaining ingredients; mix lightly. Cover; chill to blend flavors.   *Makes 6 servings*

Santa Fe Chicken Pasta Salad

12 ounces uncooked spiral pasta
2 cups cooked chicken breast cubes
½ cup chopped green onions
1 medium zucchini or yellow squash, cut
   in half lengthwise, then sliced
   crosswise
1 cup GUILTLESS GOURMET® Green
   Tomatillo Salsa
1 cup drained and coarsely chopped
   artichoke hearts
½ cup sliced black olives
   Lettuce leaves
   Fresh dill sprigs (optional)

Cook pasta according to package directions; drain.
Place pasta in large nonmetallic bowl; add chicken,
onions, zucchini, tomatillo salsa, artichoke hearts and
olives. Toss lightly. Refrigerate at least 6 hours before
serving.

To serve, line serving platter with lettuce leaves. Top
with pasta mixture. Garnish with dill, if desired.

Makes 4 servings

Lite Oriental Turkey & Pasta Salad

8 ounces uncooked capellini (angel hair pasta)
3 tablespoons lemon juice
2 tablespoons plus 1½ teaspoons vegetable oil
3 tablespoons KIKKOMAN® Lite Soy Sauce, divided
2 tablespoons minced cilantro
1¼ teaspoons Oriental sesame oil
1 teaspoon sugar
1 clove garlic, pressed
1 turkey cutlet (about ½ pound)
¼ pound snow peas, trimmed
1 carrot
1 tablespoon vegetable oil
1 tablespoon water

Cook capellini according to package directions, omitting salt. Rinse under cold water; drain thoroughly. Cool. Blend lemon juice, 2 tablespoons plus 1½ teaspoons vegetable oil, 2 tablespoons lite soy sauce, cilantro, sesame oil, sugar and garlic. Pour over capellini in bowl; toss to combine. Cover; refrigerate 30 minutes. Meanwhile, cut turkey into thin strips; cut snow peas and carrot into julienne strips. Heat remaining 1 tablespoon oil in wok or skillet over high heat. Add turkey; stir-fry 2 minutes. Add snow peas, carrot and water; stir-fry 1 minute. Stir in remaining 1 tablespoon lite soy sauce; stir to coat. Pour over capellini; toss to combine. Garnish, if desired. Serve immediately. *Makes 4 servings*

Smoked Turkey and Pepper Pasta Salad

¾ cup MIRACLE WHIP® Salad Dressing
1 tablespoon Dijon mustard
½ teaspoon dried thyme leaves
8 ounces fettuccine, cooked, drained
1 cup (8 ounces) diced LOUIS RICH®
  Hickory Smoked Breast of Turkey
¾ cup zucchini slices, cut into halves
½ cup red bell pepper strips
½ cup yellow bell pepper strips
  Salt and black pepper

• Mix salad dressing, mustard and thyme in large bowl until well blended. Add pasta, turkey and vegetables; mix lightly. Season with salt and black pepper to taste.

• Cover; refrigerate at least 1 hour before serving. Add additional salad dressing before serving, if desired.

Makes 6 servings

Oriental Turkey Noodle Salad

½ teaspoon sesame oil
½ teaspoon reduced-sodium soy sauce
1 package (3 ounces) chicken flavor
    instant oriental noodle soup mix,
    prepared according to package
    directions
¾ pound fully-cooked oven-roasted turkey
    breast, cut into ¼-inch cubes
4 ounces water chestnuts, drained and
    sliced
⅛ pound fresh snow peas, blanched*
2 large fresh mushrooms, sliced
½ cup diagonally cut carrots
2 tablespoons sliced green onion

1. In small bowl, combine sesame oil, soy sauce and prepared soup mix. Cover and refrigerate.

2. In large bowl, combine turkey, water chestnuts, snow peas, mushrooms, carrots and green onions. Fold noodles into turkey and vegetable mixture. Cover and refrigerate 2 hours.   *Serves 4*

*To blanch snow peas, plunge pea pods in boiling water 45 seconds. Immediately drain and plunge into ice water.

Favorite recipe from **National Turkey Federation**

Crab and Pasta Salad in Cantaloupe

1½ cups uncooked rotini pasta
1 cup seedless green grapes
½ cup chopped celery
½ cup fresh pineapple chunks
1 small red onion, coarsely chopped
6 ounces canned, fresh or frozen
    crabmeat, drained and rinsed
½ cup plain nonfat yogurt
¼ cup whipped salad dressing
2 tablespoons fresh lemon juice
2 tablespoons honey
2 teaspoons grated lemon peel
1 teaspoon Dijon mustard
2 small cantaloupes

1. Cook rotini according to package directions, omitting salt; drain. Rinse with cold water; drain.

2. Combine grapes, celery, pineapple, onion and crabmeat in large bowl. Combine yogurt, salad dressing, lemon juice, honey, lemon peel and mustard in small bowl. Add yogurt mixture and pasta to crabmeat mixture. Toss to coat evenly. Cover and refrigerate.

3. Cut cantaloupes in half. Remove and discard seeds. Remove some of cantaloupe with spoon, leaving a shell about ¾ inch thick. Fill cantaloupe halves with salad.

Makes 4 servings

Fresh Seafood and Linguine Salad

1½ to 3 dozens clams, scrubbed
 4 pounds mussels, scrubbed and debearded
 8 ounces linguine
   Olive oil
1½ pounds small squid, cleaned and cut
   into rings
 ¼ cup freshly squeezed lemon juice
 2 cloves garlic, minced
 ½ teaspoon salt
 ¼ teaspoon black pepper
   Additional lemon juice, salt and black
   pepper (optional)

Place clams and mussels in 1 cup boiling water in large stockpot. Cover; reduce heat to low. Steam 5 to 7 minutes until clams and mussels are opened. Discard any clams or mussels that remain closed.

Meanwhile, cook pasta according to package directions. Drain; place in large bowl and toss with 2 tablespoons olive oil.

Add just enough olive oil to large saucepan to cover bottom. Heat over medium heat; add squid. Cook and stir 2 minutes until squid is opaque. Place squid in large glass bowl. Add pasta, mussels and clams.

Combine ½ cup olive oil, ¼ cup lemon juice, garlic, ½ teaspoon salt and ¼ teaspoon pepper in small bowl; blend well. Pour over salad; toss gently to coat.

Cover; refrigerate at least 3 hours. Season with additional lemon juice, salt and pepper, if necessary.

Makes 6 servings

Seafood Orzo Salad

1 cup orzo
2 tablespoons olive oil, divided
½ pound medium shrimp, peeled and
   deveined
½ pound bay scallops
1 clove garlic, minced
2 green onions, sliced
2 tablespoons chopped fresh dill
1 tablespoon lemon juice
1 teaspoon salt
1 teaspoon TABASCO® pepper sauce

Prepare orzo according to package directions. Drain.

Meanwhile, in large skillet, heat 1 tablespoon olive oil
over medium-high heat. Add shrimp, scallops and
garlic; cook about 5 minutes or until seafood is tender,
stirring occasionally.

In large bowl, toss seafood mixture, orzo, green onions,
dill, lemon juice, salt, TABASCO® sauce and remaining
olive oil until well mixed. Serve immediately or
refrigerate to serve cold later.   *Makes 4 servings*

Albacore Salad Puttanesca with Garlic Vinaigrette

2 cups cooked, chilled angel hair pasta
2 cups chopped peeled plum tomatoes
1 can (4¼ ounces) chopped ripe olives, drained*
1 cup Garlic Vinaigrette Dressing (recipe follows)
1 can (6 ounces) STARKIST® Solid White Tuna, drained and flaked
¼ cup chopped fresh basil leaves

In large bowl, combine chilled pasta, tomatoes, olives and 1 cup Garlic Vinaigrette Dressing. Add tuna and basil leaves; toss. Serve immediately.

Makes 2 servings

*If you prefer, olives may be sliced rather than chopped.

Garlic Vinaigrette Dressing

⅓ cup red wine vinegar
2 tablespoons lemon juice
1 to 2 cloves garlic, minced or pressed
1 teaspoon ground black pepper
  Salt to taste
1 cup olive oil

In small bowl, whisk together vinegar, lemon juice, garlic, pepper and salt. Slowly add oil, whisking continuously, until well blended.

Spiral Pasta Salad

- 8 ounces tricolor spiral pasta, cooked according to package directions
- 1 can (12 ounces) STARKIST® Tuna, drained and broken into chunks
- 1 cup slivered pea pods
- 1 cup chopped yellow squash or zucchini
- 1 cup asparagus, cut into 2-inch pieces
- ½ cup slivered red onion
- ½ cup sliced pitted ripe olives

DIJON VINAIGRETTE

- ⅓ cup white wine vinegar
- ¼ cup olive or vegetable oil
- 2 tablespoons water
- 2 teaspoons Dijon mustard
- 1 teaspoon dried basil, crushed
- ¼ teaspoon pepper
  Lettuce leaves

For salad, rinse pasta in cool water; drain well. In a large bowl, toss together pasta, tuna, pea pods, squash, asparagus, onion and olives. For dressing, in a shaker jar combine remaining ingredients except lettuce. Cover and shake until well blended. Pour over salad; toss well. Serve on lettuce-lined plates.

Makes 5 servings

Party Pasta Salad

8 ounces (3 cups) bow tie pasta
¾ cup dried tart cherries
½ cup chopped carrots
½ cup chopped cucumber
¼ cup chopped green onions
¼ cup red wine vinegar
3 tablespoons vegetable oil
2 tablespoons lemon juice
2 tablespoons Dijon-style mustard
1 teaspoon dried basil leaves
½ teaspoon dried oregano leaves
¼ teaspoon dried thyme leaves
Freshly ground black pepper to taste

Cook pasta according to package directions. Drain well.
In large bowl, combine pasta, cherries, carrots,
cucumber and green onions; mix gently.

In small bowl, combine vinegar, oil, lemon juice,
mustard, basil, oregano, thyme and pepper; mix well.
Pour over pasta mixture; mix gently. Refrigerate,
covered, at least 2 hours or overnight. Mix gently
before serving.   *Makes 8 servings*

Favorite recipe from **Cherry Marketing Institute, Inc.**

Pesto Pasta Salad

2 cups firmly packed washed fresh basil
   leaves
1 cup firmly packed washed fresh parsley
¼ cup slivered almonds
¼ cup (1 ounce) grated Parmesan cheese
3 cloves garlic, coarsely chopped
½ cup FRENCH'S® Dijon Mustard
1 tablespoon FRENCH'S® Worcestershire
   Sauce
⅔ cup olive oil
4 cups cooked small pasta (about
   ½ pound uncooked), drained and
   rinsed with cold water
  Chopped seeded red bell peppers or
   tomatoes

To prepare **Dijon Pesto Sauce,** place basil, parsley, almonds, cheese and garlic in food processor. Cover and process until finely chopped. Add mustard and Worcestershire; process until well blended. Gradually add oil in steady stream, processing until thick sauce forms.

Place pasta in large bowl. Pour pesto sauce over pasta; toss well to coat evenly. Cover and refrigerate until ready to serve. Garnish with peppers.

Makes 6 side-dish servings (about 2 cups sauce)

Tangy Garlic Tortellini Salad

¼ cup mayonnaise
¼ cup plain yogurt
1 teaspoon LAWRY'S® Seasoned Pepper
1 to 1¼ teaspoons LAWRY'S® Garlic Salt
1 tablespoon plus 1½ teaspoons lemon
   juice
1 tablespoon olive oil
2 teaspoons chopped fresh chives *or*
   ¼ cup chopped green onion
9 ounces fresh cheese-filled tortellini *or*
   8 ounces spiral pasta, cooked and
   drained
1 medium-sized red bell pepper, cut into
   thin strips
1 medium zucchini, cut into julienne
   strips
2 medium carrots, cut into julienne strips

In small bowl, combine all ingredients except pasta and vegetables. In medium bowl, combine pasta and vegetables; mix lightly. Add dressing; toss lightly to coat. Refrigerate at least 30 minutes. Garnish as desired. *Makes 4 to 6 servings*

Pasta Salad in Artichoke Cups

5 cloves garlic, peeled
½ cup white wine
6 medium artichokes
1 lemon, cut into halves
6 cups chicken broth
1 tablespoon plus 1 teaspoon olive oil,
    divided
1 package (2 ounces) artichoke hearts
8 ounces corkscrew pasta or pasta twists
½ teaspoon dried basil leaves
    Basil Vinaigrette Dressing
    (page 41)

1. Place garlic and wine in small saucepan. Bring to a boil over high heat; reduce heat to low. Simmer 10 minutes.

2. Meanwhile, prepare artichokes. Cut bottoms from artichokes; remove outer leaves. Cut 1 inch off tops of artichokes. Snip tips from remaining leaves with scissors. Rub ends with lemon.

3. Bring chicken broth to a boil in Dutch oven over high heat. Add artichokes, wine mixture and 1 tablespoon oil. Reduce heat to low. Cover; simmer 25 to 30 minutes or until leaves pull easily from base. Drain.

4. Cook artichoke hearts according to package directions. Drain well. Cut into slices to make 2 cups. Set aside.

5. Cook pasta according to package directions, drain. Place pasta in large bowl. Sprinkle with remaining 1 teaspoon oil and basil.

6. Prepare Basil Vinaigrette Dressing. Add artichoke hearts and 1 cup dressing to pasta; toss gently to coat.

7. Carefully spread outer leaves of whole artichokes. Remove small heart leaves by grasping with fingers, then pulling and twisting. Scoop out fuzzy choke with spoon.

8. Fill with pasta mixture. Cover; refrigerate until serving time. Serve with remaining dressing. Garnish as desired. *Makes 6 servings*

Basil Vinaigrette Dressing

⅓ **cup white wine vinegar**
2 **tablespoons Dijon mustard**
3 **cloves garlic, peeled**
¾ **cup coarsely chopped fresh basil leaves**
1 **cup olive oil**
  Salt and black pepper to taste

1. Place vinegar, mustard and garlic in blender or food processor. Cover; process using on/off pulses until well mixed. Add basil; continue to pulse until mixture is blended.

2. With motor running, slowly pour in olive oil. Season to taste with salt and pepper.

Makes about 1½ cups

Pasta Salad with Hummus Dressing

8 ounces uncooked rigatoni, penne or
  pasta twists
3 tablespoons sesame seeds (optional)
1 (16-ounce) can chick-peas, rinsed and
  well drained
¼ cup water
¼ cup FILIPPO BERIO® Olive Oil
  Juice of 1½ lemons
3 cloves garlic, peeled
½ teaspoon ground cumin
¼ teaspoon chili powder
1 bunch green onions, trimmed, halved
  and sliced
½ green bell pepper, seeded and chopped
1 tablespoon chopped fresh Italian
  parsley
6 tablespoons mayonnaise
  Salt and freshly ground black pepper
  Ripe and green olive slivers

Preheat oven to 300°F. Cook pasta according to
package directions until al dente (tender but still firm).
Drain. Meanwhile, place sesame seeds, if desired, in
shallow pan; toast in oven until lightly browned,
stirring occasionally.

In blender container or food processor, combine
chick-peas, water, olive oil, lemon juice, garlic, cumin
and chili powder; process until mixture forms a creamy
paste. Transfer mixture to large bowl. Add green
onions, bell pepper and parsley; mix well. Add hot
pasta; toss until lightly coated with dressing. Cover;

refrigerate 30 minutes. Stir in mayonnaise. Season to taste with salt and black pepper. Sprinkle with sesame seeds; top with olives.
Makes 4 servings

Santa Fe Pasta Salad

- 8 ounces medium shell pasta (3 cups uncooked)
- 1 can (15¼ ounces) red kidney beans, drained and rinsed
- 1 can (7 ounces) corn kernels, drained
- 1 green or red bell pepper, seeded and chopped
- 1 cup (4 ounces) shredded Cheddar cheese
- ½ cup sliced black olives
- 1 bottle (8 ounces) salsa ranch salad dressing
- 2 tablespoons FRANK'S® Original REDHOT® Cayenne Pepper Sauce
- 1 teaspoon chili powder
- 3 bell peppers (green, red and/or yellow), halved and seeded (optional)

Cook pasta according to package directions; rinse in cold water and drain. Place in large bowl. Add beans, corn, chopped pepper, cheese and olives. Combine salad dressing, RedHot® Sauce and chili powder in small bowl; mix well. Pour over pasta mixture. Toss well to coat evenly. Cover and refrigerate 1 hour. Serve in pepper halves and garnish as desired.

Makes 6 side-dish servings

Simple

SELECTIONS

Ravioli Soup

1 package (9 ounces) fresh or frozen
    cheese ravioli or tortellini
¾ pound hot Italian sausage, crumbled
1 can (14½ ounces) DEL MONTE®
    FreshCut™ Diced Tomatoes with
    Basil, Garlic & Oregano
1 can (14 ounces) beef broth
1 can (14½ ounces) DEL MONTE®
    FreshCut™ Cut Green Italian Beans,
    drained
2 green onions, sliced

1. Cook pasta according to package directions; drain.

2. Meanwhile, cook sausage in 5-quart pot over
medium-high heat until no longer pink; drain. Add
tomatoes, broth and 1¾ cups water; bring to boil.

3. Reduce heat to low; stir in pasta, green beans and
green onions. Simmer until heated through. Season
with pepper and sprinkle with grated Parmesan cheese,
if desired.   *Makes 4 servings*

Minestrone Soup

1 can (14½ ounces) stewed tomatoes,
   Italian-style
2 cans (13¾ ounces each) low sodium
   chicken broth
½ cup uncooked fine egg noodles or tiny
   pasta for soup
1 can (15½ ounces) red kidney beans
3 cups BIRDS EYE® frozen Mixed
   Vegetables
   Grated Parmesan cheese

• Drain tomatoes, reserving liquid. Chop tomatoes into bite-size pieces.

• Bring broth, noodles, tomatoes and reserved liquid to boil in large saucepan over high heat. Cook, uncovered, over medium-high heat 6 minutes.

• Add beans and vegetables. Cover and cook 5 minutes or until heated through.

• Sprinkle individual servings with cheese.

Makes 4 servings

Chicken and Pasta Soup

1   (2½-pound) chicken, cut up
1   (46-fluid ounce) can COLLEGE INN®
       Chicken Broth
1   (16-ounce) can cut green beans,
       drained
1   (6-ounce) can tomato paste
1   cup uncooked small shell macaroni
1   teaspoon dried basil leaves

In large saucepan, over medium-high heat, bring
chicken and chicken broth to a boil; reduce heat.
Cover; simmer 25 minutes or until chicken is tender.
Remove chicken; cool slightly. Add remaining
ingredients to broth. Heat to a boil; reduce heat. Cover;
simmer 20 minutes or until macaroni is cooked.
Meanwhile, remove chicken from bones and cut into
bite-size pieces. Add to soup; cook 5 minutes more.

Makes 6 servings

Garden Pasta Salad

8 ounces uncooked shaped pasta
1 bag (16 ounces) BIRDS EYE® frozen
    Farm Fresh Mixtures Broccoli,
    Cauliflower and Carrots
⅔ cup Italian salad dressing
¼ cup grated Parmesan cheese
½ teaspoon garlic powder
    Lettuce leaves (optional)

• Cook pasta according to package directions; drain.

• Cook vegetables according to package directions; chill.

• Combine all ingredients in large serving bowl; mix well. Serve chilled over lettuce, if desired.

Makes 6 to 8 servings

Pepperoni Pasta Salad

1 bag (16 ounces) BIRDS EYE® frozen
    Farm Fresh Mixtures Broccoli, Red
    Peppers, Onions and Mushrooms
2 cups cooked macaroni
1 package (3 ounces) thinly sliced
    pepperoni
¼ to ½ cup peppercorn or ranch salad
    dressing

• Cook vegetables according to package directions.

• Combine vegetables and macaroni in large bowl. Chill.

• Toss with pepperoni and dressing. Add salt and pepper to taste.   *Makes 4 to 6 servings*

Bow Tie Pasta Salad

16 ounces uncooked bow ties, rotini, ziti
      or other shaped pasta
 1   bag (16 ounces) BIRDS EYE® frozen
      Farm Fresh Mixtures Broccoli,
      Cauliflower and Carrots*
 1   cup Italian, creamy Italian or favorite
      salad dressing
 1   bunch green onions, thinly sliced
 1   cup pitted ripe olives, halved (optional)

• Cook pasta according to package directions; drain.

• Cook vegetables according to package directions; drain.

• Combine pasta and vegetables with remaining ingredients in large bowl. Cover and chill until ready to serve.   *Makes about 8 side-dish servings*

*Or, substitute any other BIRDS EYE® frozen Farm Fresh Mixtures variety.

Tarragon Tuna Pasta Salad

½ cup mayonnaise
½ teaspoon dried tarragon or thyme,
   crushed
3 cups chilled cooked mostaccioli or
   elbow macaroni
2 stalks celery, sliced
1 can (6⅛ ounces) solid white tuna in
   water, drained and broken into bite-
   size pieces
1 can (14½ ounces) DEL MONTE® Peas
   and Carrots, drained

1. Combine mayonnaise and tarragon in large bowl.
Add pasta, celery and tuna. Gently stir in peas and
carrots.

2. Cover serving plates with lettuce, if desired. Top
with salad. Garnish, if desired.   *Makes 4 servings*

Healthy Hint: Use light mayonnaise instead of regular
mayonnaise.

Caesar Shrimp Pasta Salad

1 can (14½ ounces) DEL MONTE®
   FreshCut™ Diced Tomatoes with
   Garlic & Onion, undrained
1 pound cooked tiny shrimp
6 cups cooked corkscrew pasta
1 small cucumber, diced
1 cup Caesar dressing
3 green onions, sliced

1. Drain tomatoes, reserving ⅓ cup liquid. In large bowl, combine reserved tomato liquid with tomatoes and remaining ingredients. Season with salt and pepper to taste, if desired.

2. Cover and refrigerate until serving time. Garnish, if desired.   *Makes 4 servings*

Cheeseburger Macaroni

2 cups mostaccioli or elbow macaroni
1 pound ground beef
1 medium onion, chopped
1 can (14½ ounces) DEL MONTE® *FreshCut*™ Diced Tomatoes with Basil, Garlic & Oregano
¼ cup DEL MONTE® Tomato Ketchup
1 cup (4 ounces) shredded Cheddar cheese

1. Cook pasta according to package directions; drain.

2. Brown meat with onion in large skillet; drain. Season with salt and pepper, if desired. Stir in tomatoes, ketchup and pasta; heat through.

3. Top with cheese. Garnish, if desired.

Makes 4 servings

Rotini with Cauliflower and Prosciutto

8 ounces uncooked rotini pasta
1 head cauliflower, separated into florets
¼ cup FILIPPO BERIO® Extra Virgin
   Olive Oil
1 onion, thinly sliced
   Salt and freshly ground black pepper
¼ pound thinly sliced prosciutto
   (preferably imported), cut into
   bite-size pieces

Cook pasta according to package directions until
al dente (tender but still firm). Drain. In large
saucepan, cook cauliflower florets in boiling salted
water 3 to 5 minutes or until tender. Add to colander
with pasta. Drain; transfer to large bowl. In medium
saucepan, heat olive oil over medium heat until hot.
Add onion; cook and stir 5 to 7 minutes or until tender.
Add onion with olive oil to pasta mixture; toss until
lightly coated. Season to taste with salt and pepper. Top
with prosciutto.   *Makes 4 servings*

Ravioli with Tomato and Zucchini

2 packages (9 ounces each) fresh or
    frozen cheese ravioli or tortellini
¾ pound hot Italian sausage, crumbled
2 cans (14½ ounces each) DEL MONTE®
    FreshCut™ Diced Tomatoes,
    undrained
1 medium zucchini, thinly sliced and
    quartered
1 teaspoon dried basil, crushed
½ cup ricotta cheese *or* 2 tablespoons
    grated Parmesan cheese

1. Cook pasta according to package directions; drain.

2. Brown sausage in large skillet or saucepan, over medium-high heat until no longer pink; drain, reserving sausage in skillet.

3. Add tomatoes, zucchini and basil to skillet. Cook about 8 minutes or until zucchini is just tender-crisp, stirring occasionally. Season with pepper, if desired.

4. Spoon sauce over hot pasta. Top with ricotta cheese. Garnish, if desired.   *Makes 4 servings*

Angel Hair Carbonara

⅔ cup milk
2 tablespoons margarine or butter
1 package (4.8 ounces) PASTA RONI®
   Angel Hair Pasta with Herbs
2 cups chopped cooked pork or ham
1 package (10 ounces) frozen peas
¼ cup sliced green onions

1. In round 3-quart microwavable glass casserole, combine 1½ cups water, milk and margarine. Microwave, uncovered, on HIGH 4 to 5 minutes or until boiling.

2. Gradually add pasta while stirring. Separate pasta with a fork, if needed.

3. Stir in contents of seasoning packet.

4. Microwave, uncovered, on HIGH 4 minutes, stirring gently after 2 minutes. Separate pasta with a fork if needed. Stir in pork, frozen peas and onions. Continue to microwave 2 to 3 minutes. Sauce will be very thin, but will thicken upon standing.

5. Let stand 3 minutes or until desired consistency. Stir before serving.   *Makes 4 servings*

Pesto Chicken Pasta

1 tablespoon oil
2 boneless skinless chicken breast halves
   (about ¾ pound), cut into strips
1 red pepper, cut into strips
1 package (9 ounces) DI GIORNO®
   Mozzarella Garlic Tortelloni, cooked,
   drained
1 package (7 ounces) DI GIORNO®
   Pesto Sauce

HEAT oil in skillet on medium-high heat. Add chicken and pepper; cook and stir until chicken is cooked through.

TOSS with hot tortelloni and sauce.

Makes 2 to 3 servings

Creamy Chicken Fettuccine

1 jar (12 ounces) HEINZ® HomeStyle
   Classic Chicken Gravy
1 package (4 ounces) light garlic and
   herb spreadable cheese
2 cups cubed cooked chicken
4 cups hot cooked and drained spinach
   fettuccine (about 8 ounces uncooked)
   Snipped fresh chives, basil or thyme

Combine gravy and cheese in 2-quart saucepan. Cook and stir over medium heat until cheese melts and sauce is smooth. Stir in chicken; cook until heated through. Thin sauce with milk, if desired. Serve over fettuccine. Sprinkle with chives.   *Makes 4 servings*

Peppy Pesto Toss

    8 **ounces uncooked ziti or mostaccioli**
    1 **package (16 ounces) frozen bell pepper**
       and onion strips, thawed
    ½ **pound deli turkey breast or smoked**
       turkey breast, cut ½ inch thick
    1 **cup half-and-half**
    ½ **cup pesto sauce**
    ¼ **cup grated Parmesan or Asiago cheese**

1. Cook pasta according to package directions.

2. Add pepper and onion mixture to pasta water during last 2 minutes of cooking. Meanwhile, cut turkey into ½-inch cubes.

3. Drain pasta and vegetables in colander.

4. Combine half-and-half, pesto and turkey in saucepan used to prepare pasta. Cook 2 minutes or until heated through. Return pasta and vegetables to saucepan; toss well.

5. Sprinkle with cheese. Serve immediately.

Makes 4 servings

Quick Turkey Tortelloni

1 package (10 ounces) DI GIORNO®
   Alfredo or Four Cheese Sauce
1 package (10 ounces) frozen chopped
   broccoli, thawed, drained *or* 2 cups
   broccoli flowerets, cooked tender-
   crisp, drained
½ pound cooked turkey, cut into strips
   (about 1½ cups)
1 jar (2½ ounces) sliced mushrooms,
   drained (optional)
1 package (9 ounces) DI GIORNO®
   Mushroom or Mozzarella Garlic
   Tortelloni, cooked, drained
   Toasted sliced almonds (optional)

HEAT sauce, broccoli, turkey and mushrooms in saucepan on medium heat.

SPOON over hot tortelloni. Sprinkle with almonds.

Makes 3 to 4 servings

Tuna Linguine

1 (6½-ounce) can white albacore tuna, packed in water
6 tablespoons FILIPPO BERIO® Extra-Virgin Flavorful Olive Oil
Juice of 1 lemon
½ cup chopped fresh parsley
¼ teaspoon black pepper
¼ teaspoon salt, optional
¾ pound uncooked linguine (or any other pasta)

1. Drain tuna. In small bowl, break tuna into chunks; add oil. Stir in lemon juice, parsley, pepper and salt until combined.

2. Cook pasta according to package directions; do not overcook. Drain.

3. Spoon tuna sauce over pasta in large bowl; toss gently to coat. Serve.

Makes 4 servings

Shrimp & Asparagus Fettuccine

12 ounces uncooked fettuccine
1 box (10 ounces) BIRDS EYE® frozen
   Asparagus Cuts*
1 tablespoon vegetable oil
1 package (16 ounces) frozen, uncooked
   cocktail-size shrimp
1 jar (12 ounces) prepared alfredo sauce
1 jar (4 ounces) sliced pimiento, drained

• Cook fettuccine according to package directions, adding asparagus to water 8 minutes before pasta is cooked. Drain.

• Meanwhile, heat oil in large skillet over medium-high heat. Add shrimp; cover and cook 3 minutes or until shrimp turn pink.

• Drain excess liquid, leaving shrimp and about 2 tablespoons liquid in skillet. Reduce heat to low.

• Stir in alfredo sauce and pimiento; cover and cook 5 minutes. *Do not boil.*

• Toss fettuccine and asparagus with shrimp mixture.

Makes about 4 servings

*Or, substitute 1½ cups BIRDS EYE® frozen Green Peas or BIRDS EYE® frozen Broccoli Cuts.

Noodles Romanoff

1   package (8 ounces) wide egg noodles,
    cooked and drained
1½ cups prepared HIDDEN VALLEY
    RANCH® Original Ranch® salad
    dressing
¼   cup sour cream
¼   cup grated Parmesan cheese

Preheat oven to 350°F. Place noodles in greased
2-quart baking dish; mix in salad dressing, sour cream
and cheese. Bake until heated through, about 15
minutes. Garnish with additional Parmesan cheese, if
desired. Serve immediately.   *Serves 4 to 6*

Variations: Mix 1 cup prepared Hidden Valley Ranch®
Original Ranch® salad dressing and 2 cups cooked,
drained pasta with tiny cooked shrimp; cubed cooked
beef with sautéed sliced mushrooms; or stir-fried
vegetables, such as broccoli flowerets, cauliflowerets,
zucchini and tomatoes.

Salmon Tortellini

1   package (7 ounces) cheese-filled
      tortellini, cooked and drained
1   container (8 ounces) PHILADELPHIA
      BRAND® Soft Cream Cheese with
      Smoked Salmon
½   cup finely chopped cucumber
1   teaspoon dried dill weed *or* 2 teaspoons
      fresh dill

• Lightly toss hot tortellini with remaining
ingredients. Serve immediately.

Makes 6 to 8 servings

Easy Macaroni and Cheese

1   (46-fluid ounce) can COLLEGE INN®
      Chicken or Beef Broth
1   (12-ounce) package uncooked spiral
      macaroni
½   cup margarine, divided
¼   cup all-purpose flour
2   cups (8 ounces) shredded Cheddar
      cheese
30 RITZ® Crackers, coarsely crushed

In large heavy saucepan, heat broth to a boil; add
macaroni and cook according to package directions,
omitting salt. Drain, reserving 2 cups broth (if
necessary, add water). Set aside.

In medium saucepan, over medium-high heat, melt ¼ cup margarine. Blend in flour. Gradually add reserved broth, stirring constantly until mixture thickens and boils. Cook and stir 2 minutes. Stir in cheese until melted. Combine cheese sauce and macaroni in 2-quart casserole. Melt remaining ¼ cup margarine; stir in cracker crumbs. Sprinkle over macaroni mixture. Bake at 400°F for 30 minutes or until hot.

Makes 6 to 8 servings

Quick Chili Bake

1 **can (15 to 16 ounces) chili**
1 **jar (12 ounces) chunky salsa**
1 **can (12 ounces) corn, drained**
8 **ounces MUELLER'S® Twists (about 4 cups), cooked 5 minutes and drained**
½ **cup (2 ounces) shredded Cheddar cheese**

1. In large bowl, combine chili, salsa and corn. Add pasta; toss to coat. Spoon into 2-quart casserole; top with cheese.

2. Bake in 400°F oven 30 minutes or until heated. If desired, serve with corn chips.   *Makes 6 servings*

Spinach Pesto

1 box (10 ounces) BIRDS EYE® frozen
    Chopped or Whole Leaf Spinach
2 tablespoons dried basil
1 large clove garlic, peeled
⅓ cup walnuts (optional)
⅓ cup grated Parmesan cheese
⅓ to ½ cup olive or vegetable oil
    Hot cooked pasta

• Cook spinach according to package directions; place in strainer. Press excess water from spinach with back of spoon. Chill.

• Combine spinach, basil, garlic, walnuts and cheese in food processor;* process until well blended.

• Add oil slowly to mixture with machine running. Cover pesto and chill until needed. Serve over pasta.

Makes about 1¼ cups

*To prepare pesto in blender, combine all ingredients in blender; blend until well mixed, scraping down sides of blender if necessary.

Creamy Fettuccine Alfredo

1 (8-ounce) package PHILADELPHIA
    BRAND® Cream Cheese, cubed
¾ cup (3 ounces) KRAFT® 100% Grated
    Parmesan Cheese
½ cup butter or margarine
½ cup milk
8 ounces uncooked fettuccine, cooked,
    drained and kept warm

In large saucepan, combine cream cheese, Parmesan cheese, butter and milk; stir over low heat until smooth. Add fettuccine; toss lightly.

Makes 4 servings

Fettuccine Alfeta

12 ounces fettuccine
3 tablespoons olive oil
1 package (8 ounces) ATHENOS® Feta
    Cheese with Basil & Tomato,
    crumbled
2 cups chopped tomatoes
¼ cup julienne-cut fresh basil *or*
    2 teaspoons dried basil leaves,
    crushed
    Fresh ground pepper and salt

COOK fettuccine 8 to 10 minutes or until al dente; drain. Return to pan; toss with oil.

TOSS with feta cheese, tomatoes and basil. Season to taste with pepper and salt.   *Makes 6 servings*

Variation: Substitute ATHENOS® Feta Cheese with Garlic & Herb for ATHENOS® Feta Cheese with Basil & Tomato.

Fettuccine with Fresh Herb and Parmesan Sauce

8 ounces uncooked fettuccine noodles
3 tablespoons grated Parmesan or
   pecorino cheese
3 tablespoons FILIPPO BERIO® Extra
   Virgin Olive Oil
2 tablespoons chopped fresh herbs*
   (basil, oregano or chives)
1 egg yolk**
½ clove garlic, crushed
   Salt and freshly ground pepper

Cook pasta according to package directions until al dente (tender but still firm). Drain. Meanwhile, in small bowl, combine cheese, olive oil, herbs, egg yolk and garlic.

Return pasta to saucepan; place over very low heat. Pour olive oil mixture over pasta; toss until lightly coated. (Do not overheat mixture—sauce will coat pasta quickly.) Season to taste with salt and pepper.

Makes 2 servings

*Omit herbs if fresh are unavailable. Do not substitute dried herbs.
**Use Grade A clean, uncracked egg.

Cheesy Herb-Stuffed Mushrooms with Spinach Fettuccine

  2 packages (9 ounces each) fresh spinach
     fettuccine
 ⅓ cup extra-virgin olive oil
  1 tablespoon dried basil leaves
  2 cloves garlic, minced
  1 package (6½ ounces) garlic and herb
     soft spreadable cheese
 16 large mushrooms, rinsed and stems
     removed

1. Prepare barbecue grill for direct cooking.

2. Cook fettuccine according to package directions. Drain; return to saucepan.

3. Meanwhile, combine oil, basil and garlic in small bowl; pour over cooked pasta. Toss well; set aside.

4. Cut aluminum foil into 4 large squares. Spoon about 1 tablespoon cheese into each mushroom cap. Place four mushroom caps, cheese side up, in center of each square. Fold aluminum foil to close, leaving small air pocket directly above cheese.

5. Place packets on grid. Grill, on covered grill, over hot coals 5 minutes or until mushroom caps are fork-tender. Remove from grill.

6. Transfer fettuccine to serving bowl. Remove mushroom caps from packets; arrange over fettuccine. Serve immediately.   *Makes 4 to 6 servings*

Cheese Stuffed Shells with Basil

- 1 cup (8 ounces) low-fat ricotta cheese
- 1 (8-ounce) package HEALTHY CHOICE®
  Fat Free natural shredded Mozzarella
  Cheese
- 1 cup chopped fresh basil
- 2 teaspoons minced fresh garlic
- 6 ounces (16 shells) jumbo pasta shells,
  cooked
- 1 (26-ounce) jar HEALTHY CHOICE®
  Traditional Pasta Sauce

Heat oven to 350°F. In large bowl, stir together ricotta cheese, 1 cup mozzarella cheese, basil and garlic. Fill each shell with about 2 tablespoons cheese filling. Place in 12×7-inch baking dish sprayed with nonstick cooking spray. Pour sauce over filled shells. Sprinkle with remaining mozzarella cheese. Cover and bake at 350°F, 20 to 25 minutes. *Makes 8 servings*

Linguine with Oil and Garlic

- ½ cup FILIPPO BERIO® Extra-Virgin
  Flavorful Olive Oil, divided
- 10 cloves garlic, minced
- ¾ pound uncooked linguine
- ¼ teaspoon pepper
- ¼ teaspoon salt (optional)

1. Heat 2 tablespoons olive oil in small saucepan over medium heat. Add garlic; cook and stir until lightly browned. Remove from heat; set aside.

2. Cook linguine according to package directions until tender. Do not overcook.

3. Drain pasta; return to saucepan. Toss with garlic and olive oil mixture, remaining 6 tablespoons olive oil, pepper and salt, if desired.   *Makes 4 servings*

Tortellini with Artichokes, Olives and Feta Cheese

    2 **packages (9 ounces) refrigerated cheese-filled spinach tortellini**
    2 **jars (4 ounces) marinated artichoke heart quarters, drained***
    2 **medium carrots, sliced diagonally**
  ½ **cup sliced pitted ripe olives**
  ½ **cup (2 ounces) crumbled feta cheese**
  ½ **cup cheese-garlic Italian salad dressing**

1. Cook pasta according to package directions. Remove and rinse well under cold water until pasta is cool.

2. Combine pasta, artichoke hearts, carrots, olives and feta cheese in large bowl. Add salad dressing; toss lightly. Season to taste with pepper.

Makes 6 servings

*For additional flavor, add artichoke marinade to tortellini along with salad dressing.

Rigatoni with Broccoli

8 ounces uncooked rigatoni pasta

1 bunch fresh broccoli, trimmed and
  separated into florets with 1-inch
  stems

1 tablespoon FILIPPO BERIO® Extra
  Virgin Olive Oil

1 clove garlic, minced
  Crushed red pepper
  Grated Parmesan cheese

Cook pasta according to package directions until
al dente (tender but still firm). Add broccoli during last
5 minutes of cooking time; cook until broccoli is
tender-crisp. Drain pasta and broccoli; transfer to large
bowl. Meanwhile, in small skillet, heat olive oil over
medium heat until hot. Add garlic; cook and stir 1 to 2
minutes or until golden. Pour oil mixture over hot
pasta mixture; toss until lightly coated. Season to taste
with pepper. Top with cheese. *Makes 3 to 4 servings*

Pasta Primavera

8 ounces uncooked mafalde

2 medium zucchini (about 1 pound)

3 tablespoons roasted garlic-flavored
  vegetable oil

1 red bell pepper, thinly sliced

½ cup loosely packed fresh basil leaves,
  coarsely chopped

½ cup grated Parmesan cheese

1. Cook pasta according to package directions; drain. Place in large bowl.

2. While pasta is cooking, cut zucchini lengthwise into halves. Cut crosswise into thin slices.

3. Heat oil in large skillet over medium-high heat until hot. Add zucchini and bell pepper; cook and stir 3 to 4 minutes or until vegetables are crisp-tender, stirring frequently.

4. Add zucchini mixture and basil to pasta; toss gently until well combined. Season to taste with salt and black pepper. Serve with cheese.   *Makes 4 servings*

Quick Tortellini with Artichokes

- 1   **package (9 ounces) DI GIORNO®**
  Cheese Tortellini or Mozzarella Garlic
  Tortellini, cooked, drained
- 1   **can (14 ounces) artichoke hearts,**
  drained, quartered
- ½   **red pepper, cut into thin strips**
- 1   **green onion, thinly sliced**
- 1   **package (7 ounces) DI GIORNO® Pesto**
  Sauce or Olive Oil and Garlic Sauce

PLACE all ingredients except sauce in large bowl.

STIR sauce. Add to tortellini mixture; mix lightly. Serve immediately or refrigerate. Let refrigerated mixture stand at room temperature 30 minutes before serving; toss before serving.   *Makes 4 servings*

Fusilli with Broccoli Rabe

8 ounces uncooked fusilli pasta
1 pound broccoli rabe, trimmed and cut
    into 1-inch pieces
⅓ cup FILIPPO BERIO® Extra Virgin
    Olive Oil
1 clove garlic, minced
    Salt and freshly ground black pepper
    Grated pecornio cheese

Cook pasta according to package directions until
al dente (tender but still firm). Drain. In large
saucepan, cook broccoli rabe in boiling salted water
3 minutes or until tender. Add to colander with pasta.
Drain; transfer to large bowl. In small saucepan, heat
olive oil over medium heat until hot. Add garlic; cook
and stir 30 seconds to 1 minute or until golden. Add to
pasta mixture; toss until well coated. Season to taste
with salt and pepper. Top with cheese.

Makes 3 to 4 servings

Thai Noodles with Peanut Sauce

2   packages (3 ounces each) Oriental
      flavor instant ramen noodles
2   cups BIRDS EYE® frozen Farm Fresh
      Mixtures Broccoli, Carrots and Water
      Chestnuts
⅓   cup hot water
¼   cup creamy peanut butter
1   teaspoon sugar
⅛   to ¼ teaspoon crushed red pepper flakes

• Reserve seasoning packets from noodles.

• Bring 4 cups water to a boil in large saucepan. Add
noodles and vegetables. Cook 3 minutes, stirring
occasionally; drain.

• Meanwhile, whisk together hot water, peanut butter,
sugar, red pepper flakes and reserved seasoning packets
in large bowl until blended.

• Add noodles and vegetables; toss to coat. Serve warm.

Makes about 4 servings

Springtime Pasta

12 ounces uncooked fettuccine or other
   long pasta
1 bag (16 ounces) BIRDS EYE® frozen
   Farm Fresh Mixtures Cauliflower,
   Carrots and Snow Pea Pods
⅓ cup creamy Caesar, Italian or ranch
   salad dressing
1 teaspoon dried basil
1 teaspoon garlic powder
⅓ cup grated Parmesan cheese

• Cook pasta according to package directions; drain.

• Cook vegetables according to package directions.

• Combine pasta, vegetables, dressing and spices in
large skillet; mix well.

• Cook over medium heat just until heated through.

• Add cheese; toss to coat pasta. Add salt and pepper to
taste.   *Makes 4 to 6 servings*

Spaghetti with Garlic

12 ounces uncooked spaghetti
4½ teaspoons FILIPPO BERIO®
   Olive Oil
1 clove garlic, sliced
   Salt and freshly ground black pepper
   Grated Parmesan cheese

Cook pasta according to package directions until al dente (tender but still firm). Drain; transfer to large bowl. In small skillet, heat olive oil over medium heat until hot. Add garlic; cook and stir 2 to 3 minutes or until golden. Discard garlic. Pour oil over hot pasta; toss until lightly coated. Season to taste with salt and pepper. Top with cheese.   *Makes 4 servings*

Red Pepper Pasta

1 **cup prepared HIDDEN VALLEY RANCH®**
   Ranch Italian salad dressing
¼ **cup bottled roasted red peppers or**
   pimientos
½ **pound fresh mushrooms, halved or**
   sliced
6 **ounces angel hair pasta, cooked and**
   drained
   Cracked black pepper to taste
   Watercress or parsley sprigs

In blender, combine salad dressing and red peppers; blend until almost smooth. In large bowl, pour mixture over mushrooms, tossing gently to coat. Add pasta to mushroom mixture; toss again. Season with black pepper. Garnish with watercress.   *Serves 4*

Ditalini with Zucchini

8 ounces uncooked ditalini pasta
¼ cup FILIPPO BERIO® Olive Oil
1 pound zucchini, trimmed and cut into
    thin rounds
1 onion, thinly sliced
1 tomato
1 tablespoon minced fresh parsley
    Salt and freshly ground black pepper

Cook pasta according to package directions until
al dente (tender but still firm). Drain. In medium
skillet, heat olive oil over medium heat until hot. Add
zucchini and onion; cook and stir 10 minutes or until
zucchini is tender-crisp. Place tomato in small
saucepan of boiling water; boil 1 minute. Place in bowl
of ice water for 10 seconds. Remove skin with paring
knife; chop tomato. In large bowl, combine zucchini
mixture, tomato and parsley. Toss with pasta. Season to
taste with salt and pepper.   *Makes 3 to 4 servings*

Vegetable Macaroni & Cheese

1 box (14 ounces) macaroni and cheese
1 bag (16 ounces) BIRDS EYE® frozen
    Farm Fresh Mixtures Broccoli,
    Cauliflower and Carrots*

• Prepare macaroni and cheese according to package
directions.

• Add vegetables during last 5 minutes of cooking time. Continue preparing recipe according to package directions.   *Makes about 4 servings*

*Or, substitute any other BIRDS EYE® frozen Farm Fresh Mixtures variety.

Easy Cheesy Tomato Macaroni

    2 packages (7 ounces *each*) macaroni and
         cheese dinner
    1 tablespoon olive or vegetable oil
    1 cup (1 small) finely chopped onion
    1 cup (2 large stalks) thinly sliced celery
   3½ cups (28-ounce can) CONTADINA®
         Dalla Casa Buitoni Crushed
         Tomatoes
         Grated Parmesan cheese (optional)
         Sliced green onion or celery leaves
         (optional)

COOK macaroni (from macaroni and cheese dinner) according to package directions; drain. Heat oil in large skillet over medium-high heat. Add onion and celery; cook for 3 minutes or until tender.

COMBINE tomatoes and cheese mix (from macaroni and cheese dinner) in small bowl; mix well. Stir into onion-celery mixture. Cook, stirring constantly, for 2 minutes or until mixture thickens. Stir in macaroni.

SPRINKLE with Parmesan cheese and green onion; serve.   *Makes 6 to 8 servings*

Pasta

TOPPERS

Burgundy Beef Pasta

8 ounces uncooked linguine
1 pound top sirloin, very thinly sliced
   crosswise
2 cloves garlic, minced
½ teaspoon dried thyme leaves, crushed
2 teaspoons vegetable oil
¼ pound fresh mushrooms, sliced
1 can (14½ ounces) DEL MONTE®
   Stewed Tomatoes (No Salt Added)
1 can (8 ounces) DEL MONTE® Tomato
   Sauce (No Salt Added)
¾ cup dry red wine
   Chopped parsley (optional)

1. Cook pasta according to package directions; drain.

2. Cook sirloin, garlic and thyme in oil in large skillet over medium-high heat 3 minutes.

3. Add mushrooms; cook 1 minute.

4. Add tomatoes, tomato sauce and wine. Cook, uncovered, over medium heat 15 minutes, stirring occasionally.

5. Serve over pasta. Garnish with chopped parsley, if desired.   *Makes 4 servings*

Hint: Cook pasta ahead; rinse and drain. Cover and refrigerate. Just before serving, heat in microwave or dip in boiling water.

Pasta Primavera with Italian Sausage

1 package (8 ounces) dried CONTADINA®
   Dalla Casa Buitoni Linguine, cooked,
   drained and kept warm
2 teaspoons olive oil
8 ounces mild Italian sausage links,
   casings removed
1 cup (1 large) sliced zucchini
2 cups (17-ounce can) CONTADINA®
   Dalla Casa Buitoni Country Italian
   Cooking Sauce with Mushrooms &
   Roasted Garlic
   Chopped fresh parsley

HEAT oil in large skillet over medium-high heat. Add
sausage; cook for 6 to 8 minutes or until no longer
pink. Remove; cut into bite-size pieces. Drain, leaving
1 tablespoon drippings.

ADD zucchini to skillet; cook for 2 minutes or until
tender. Stir in cooking sauce and sausage; cook for 5 to
7 minutes or until flavors are blended.

STIR pasta into sauce. Sprinkle with parsley before
serving.   *Makes 4 servings*

Sausage Spaghetti

1 pound **BOB EVANS FARMS**® **Original Recipe or Italian Roll Sausage**
1 large onion, chopped
2 cloves garlic, minced
1 (6-ounce) can tomato paste
1 (32-ounce) can whole tomatoes (regular or Italian style), undrained
1 (4-ounce) can mushroom stems and pieces, drained
1 tablespoon Worcestershire sauce
2 tablespoons Italian seasoning or to taste
1 pound spaghetti, cooked according to package directions and drained
    Grated Parmesan cheese

Crumble sausage into large skillet. Add onion and garlic. Cook over medium heat until sausage is browned, stirring occasionally. Drain off any drippings. Stir in tomato paste; cook 3 minutes. Add all remaining ingredients except spaghetti and cheese, stirring well to break up tomatoes. Bring to a boil over high heat. Reduce heat to low; simmer 30 minutes, stirring occasionally. Adjust seasonings, if desired. Pour over hot spaghetti. Serve with cheese. Refrigerate leftovers.   *Makes 6 servings*

Pasta with Sausage and Mustard Sauce

- 1 cup BLUE DIAMOND® Blanched Slivered Almonds
- 5 tablespoons olive oil, divided
- 2 red or green bell peppers, diced
- 1 pound Italian sausage, casing removed
- 3 cloves garlic, chopped finely
- 2 tablespoons chopped fresh basil *or* 1 teaspoon dried basil
- ¾ cup dry white wine
- ¾ cup heavy cream
- 1½ tablespoons Dijon mustard
- ¼ teaspoon pepper
- 1 pound fresh pasta *or* 8 ounces dried pasta, cooked

Sauté almonds in 1 tablespoon oil until golden; reserve. Add remaining 4 tablespoons oil to pan. Sauté bell peppers and sausage until bell peppers are just tender and sausage is browned and crumbly, about 3 minutes. Stir in garlic, basil, wine and cream. Cook over high heat until liquid thickens and coats the back of a spoon, about 3 minutes. Stir in mustard and pepper. Add almonds. Toss with hot cooked pasta.

Makes 4 to 6 servings

Bolognese Sauce

1 pound dried pasta, cooked, drained and kept warm
1 pound mild Italian sausage
1¾ cups (15-ounce can) CONTADINA® Dalla Casa Buitoni Tomato Puree
1¾ cups (14.5-ounce can) CONTADINA® Dalla Casa Buitoni Recipe Ready Diced Tomatoes, undrained
¾ cup beef broth or wine
⅔ cup CONTADINA® Dalla Casa Buitoni Italian Paste with Roasted Garlic
½ teaspoon salt (optional)
   Grated Parmesan cheese

COOK sausage in large skillet over medium-high heat, stirring to break up sausage, for 4 to 5 minutes or until no longer pink; drain. Add tomato puree, tomatoes and juice, broth, tomato paste and salt; bring to a boil. Reduce heat to low; cook for 10 to 15 minutes.

SERVE over pasta; sprinkle with cheese.

Makes 6 to 8 servings

Chunky Pasta Sauce with Meat

6 ounces ground beef
6 ounces mild or hot Italian sausage,
   sliced
½ medium onion, coarsely chopped
1 clove garlic, minced
2 cans (14½ ounces each) DEL MONTE®
   FreshCut™ Diced Tomatoes with
   Basil, Garlic & Oregano
1 can (8 ounces) DEL MONTE® Tomato
   Sauce
¼ cup red wine, optional
   Hot cooked pasta
   Grated Parmesan cheese

1. Brown beef and sausage in large saucepan; drain all but 1 tablespoon drippings.

2. Add onion and garlic; cook until tender. Add undrained tomatoes, tomato sauce and wine.

3. Boil, uncovered, 15 minutes, stirring frequently. Serve over pasta; top with Parmesan cheese.

Makes 4 servings (4 cups sauce)

Lamb with Yogurt Mint Sauce

¾ pound boneless lamb or beef, cut into
      ¼-inch cubes
1 tablespoon olive oil
1 medium onion, cut into wedges
1 can (14½ ounces) DEL MONTE®
      FreshCut™ Diced Tomatoes,
      undrained
1 to 2 tablespoons chutney
1 teaspoon ground cumin
⅓ cup plain nonfat yogurt
1 tablespoon chopped fresh mint *or*
      1 teaspoon dried mint
4 cups hot cooked pasta

1. Brown meat in hot oil in large skillet, over medium-high heat. Stir in onion and cook 3 to 4 minutes or until tender. Add tomatoes, chutney and cumin; cook until thickened.

2. Combine yogurt with mint. Spoon meat mixture over hot pasta and top with yogurt mixture.

Makes 4 servings

Thai Meatballs and Noodles

1 pound bok choy
1 small piece fresh ginger
   (about 1 × ½ inch)
1 medium carrot, peeled
   Thai Meatballs (page 88)
12 ounces uncooked egg noodles
2 cans (13¾ ounces each) reduced
   sodium chicken broth
2 tablespoons packed brown sugar
2 tablespoons fish sauce or reduced
   sodium soy sauce
½ cup slivered fresh mint or basil leaves
   or chopped cilantro
   Red pepper curls for garnish

1. Cut off root end of bok choy with chef's knife and discard. Separate stalks; rinse well and drain.

2. Stack several stalks of bok choy; slice leaves and stalks crosswise into ½-inch-wide strips. Repeat with remaining stalks.

3. Peel ginger with vegetable peeler. Cut ginger crosswise into thin slices with paring knife. Stack slices; cut into slivers.

4. To cut carrot into julienne strips, cut lengthwise strip from carrot so it can lie flat on cutting board. Cut carrot into 2-inch lengths. Lay each piece, flat side down, on board. Cut lengthwise with utility knife into thin slices. Stack several slices; cut lengthwise through stack into ⅛- to ¼-inch-wide strips. Repeat with remaining slices.

5. Prepare Thai Meatballs.

6. While meatballs are cooking, bring 6 cups water to a boil in large saucepan over high heat. Add noodles; cook according to package directions. Drain in colander; transfer to large serving bowl.

7. Heat chicken broth in large saucepan or wok over high heat. Add brown sugar, fish sauce and ginger; stir until sugar is dissolved.

8. Add meatballs and carrots to saucepan; bring to a boil. Reduce heat to medium-low; cover and simmer 15 minutes or until meatballs are heated through.

9. Add bok choy; simmer 4 to 5 minutes or until stalks are crisp-tender. Stir in mint; pour mixture over noodles in serving bowl. Garnish, if desired.

Makes 6 servings

Thai Meatballs

1½ pounds ground beef or pork
¼ cup chopped fresh basil leaves
¼ cup chopped fresh mint leaves
2 tablespoons finely chopped fresh ginger
4 teaspoons fish sauce
6 cloves garlic, minced
1 teaspoon ground cinnamon
½ teaspoon fennel seeds, crushed
½ teaspoon pepper
2 tablespoons peanut oil, divided

1. Combine beef, basil, mint, ginger, fish sauce, garlic, cinnamon, fennel and pepper in large bowl; mix with hands or spoon until well blended.

2. Rub cutting board with 1 tablespoon oil. Pat meat mixture into 12×8-inch rectangle on board. Cut lengthwise into 4 strips with sharp knife; cut crosswise into 8 strips to form 32 squares. Shape each square into a ball.

3. Heat remaining 1 tablespoon oil in large skillet or wok over medium-high heat. Add meatballs in single layer; cook 8 to 10 minutes or until no longer pink in center, turning to brown all sides. (Cook in several batches.)

4. Remove meatballs with slotted spoon to paper towels; drain. (Meatballs may be cooled, covered and refrigerated up to 2 days in advance or frozen for longer storage. Thaw before adding to broth.)

Makes 32 meatballs

Fettuccine Romano Aldana

6 ounces plain fettuccine, cooked and drained
6 ounces spinach fettuccine, cooked and drained
¾ cup butter, divided
8 ounces mushrooms, sliced
⅔ cup chopped green onions with tops
2½ cups heavy cream, divided
1½ cups (6 ounces) grated Wisconsin Romano cheese, divided
¼ teaspoon ground nutmeg
⅛ pound prosciutto ham slices, julienne cut
White pepper

Melt ¼ cup butter in large skillet over medium-high heat. Add mushrooms and onions; cook and stir until tender. Remove from skillet; set aside. Add remaining ½ cup butter to skillet; heat until lightly browned. Add 1 cup cream; bring to a boil. Reduce heat to low; simmer until slightly thickened, about 5 minutes. Add pasta, 1 cup cream, 1 cup cheese and nutmeg; mix lightly. Combine remaining cream and cheese with mushroom mixture and prosciutto. Pour over hot pasta mixture; toss lightly. Season with pepper to taste.

Makes 4 to 6 servings

Favorite recipe from **Wisconsin Milk Marketing Board**

Veal Sauce Lucia

2 tablespoons vegetable oil
1½ pounds veal stew meat, cut into small
cubes
1 medium onion, chopped
1 medium carrot, grated
¾ teaspoon dried basil leaves
¾ teaspoon LAWRY'S® Garlic Powder with
Parsley
1 package (1.42 ounces) LAWRY'S® Extra
Rich & Thick Spaghetti Sauce Spices
& Seasoning
1¾ cups water
1 can (6 ounces) tomato paste
½ cup frozen peas
8 ounces linguine or other pasta, cooked
and drained

In Dutch oven, heat oil. Brown veal; drain fat. Add
onion, carrot, basil and Garlic Powder with Parsley;
sauté 5 minutes. Add Extra Rich & Thick Spaghetti
Sauce Seasoning Blend, water and tomato paste; blend
well. Bring to a boil. Reduce heat; simmer, covered, 30
minutes. Add peas; simmer 5 minutes.

Makes 4 servings

Presentation: Ladle sauce over cooked linguine and
serve with a Caesar salad and garlic bread.

Creamy Herbed Chicken

1   package (9 ounces) fresh bow tie pasta
      or fusilli*
1   tablespoon vegetable oil
2   boneless skinless chicken breasts
      (about 1 pound), halved and cut into
      ½-inch strips
1   small red onion, cut into slices
1   package (10 ounces) frozen green peas,
      thawed, drained
1   yellow or red pepper, cut into strips
½   cup chicken broth
1   container (8 ounces) soft cream cheese
      with garlic and herbs
      Salt and black pepper

Cook pasta in lightly salted boiling water according to package directions, about 5 minutes; drain.

Meanwhile, heat oil in large skillet or wok over medium-high heat. Add chicken and onion; stir-fry 3 minutes or until chicken is no longer pink in center. Add peas and yellow pepper; stir-fry 4 minutes. Reduce heat to medium.

Stir in broth and cream cheese. Cook, stirring constantly, until cream cheese is melted. Combine pasta and chicken mixture in serving bowl; mix lightly. Season with salt and black pepper to taste. Garnish as desired.   *Makes 4 servings*

*Substitute dried bow tie pasta or fusilli for fresh pasta. Cooking time will be longer; follow package directions.

Pasta in the Springtime

1¼ cups vegetable broth, divided
2 tablespoons cornstarch
¼ cup rice vinegar
¼ cup soy sauce
3 cloves garlic, minced
1 tablespoon sugar
1 tablespoon minced fresh ginger
1 tablespoon lemon juice
2 teaspoons sesame oil
2 teaspoons hot pepper sauce
1 teaspoon black pepper
½ pound cooked chicken breast, cut into
    matchstick-size strips
2 carrots, peeled and cut into matchstick-
    size strips
¼ pound asparagus, diagonally sliced into
    1-inch pieces
1 cup packed chopped spinach
1 pound linguine, cooked and drained

1. Combine ¼ cup vegetable broth and cornstarch in small bowl; set aside.

2. Combine remaining 1 cup vegetable broth, vinegar, soy sauce, garlic, sugar, ginger, lemon juice, sesame oil, pepper sauce and black pepper in medium saucepan. Bring to a boil over high heat. Gradually add cornstarch mixture to saucepan, stirring constantly. Bring to a boil, stirring constantly. Reduce heat; simmer 2 to 3 minutes.

3. Add chicken, carrots, asparagus and spinach to saucepan; increase heat to medium. Cook 3 minutes. Combine sauce with linguine in large bowl; stir gently.

Makes 6 servings

Speedy Ziti

- 1 **pound ziti, mostaccioli or other medium pasta shape, uncooked**
- 2 **teaspoons butter or margarine**
- 1 **medium onion, chopped**
- 1 **tablespoon Dijon mustard**
- 2 **tablespoons all-purpose flour**
- 2 **cups low-sodium chicken broth**
- ¼ **cup lemon juice**
- 1 **(10-ounce) package frozen peas, thawed and drained**
- ¼ **cup chopped fresh parsley**
- 12 **ounces chopped cooked chicken**
  Salt and pepper to taste

Prepare pasta according to package directions. While pasta is cooking, melt butter over medium heat in large skillet. Add onion and cook 3 minutes. Stir in Dijon mustard and flour. Very gradually whisk in chicken broth. Bring broth to a boil and stir in lemon juice, peas and parsley.

When pasta is done, drain well. Toss pasta and chicken with sauce; season to taste with salt and pepper.

Makes 4 servings

Favorite recipe from **National Pasta Association**

Sweety Meaty Sauce for Ziti

2 tablespoons CHEF PAUL
   PRUDHOMME'S® POULTRY
   MAGIC®, divided
1 pound ground turkey
2 tablespoons olive oil
2 tablespoons margarine
1 cup chopped onion
1 cup chopped green bell pepper
2 cups canned crushed tomatoes
1 cup tomato purée
¾ cup diced carrots
1½ cups chicken stock or water, divided
1 tablespoon granulated sugar
½ teaspoon salt
1 tablespoon dark brown sugar, optional
12 ounces ziti pasta, cooked and drained

Mix 1 tablespoon plus 2 teaspoons Poultry Magic® with
turkey, working it in well with your hands; set aside.

Heat oil and margarine in 3½-quart saucepan over
medium-high heat 1 minute or until margarine has
melted and mixture begins to sizzle. Add turkey; cook,
stirring occasionally to separate chunks, until turkey is
no longer pink, about 6 minutes. Add onion and green
bell pepper; cook and stir 3 to 4 minutes or until
tender. Add the remaining 1 teaspoon Poultry Magic®,
tomatoes, tomato purée, carrots, ½ cup stock,
granulated sugar and salt; mix well. (If you like a
sweeter sauce, add brown sugar.) Cook, stirring

occasionally, 3 to 4 minutes or until mixture comes to a boil. Reduce heat to medium-low; cover. Simmer 30 minutes, stirring occasionally. Stir in remaining 1 cup stock; cover. Simmer an additional 20 minutes or until sauce has thickened and has changed from bright red to dark red in color, stirring occasionally. Remove from heat. Serve over hot pasta.   *Makes 4 servings*

Quick Chicken Marinara

1 tablespoon olive oil
2 boneless skinless chicken breasts
    halves (about ¾ pound), cut into
    strips
1 yellow or green pepper, cut into strips
1 package (15 ounces) DI GIORNO®
    Marinara Sauce
1 package (9 ounces) DI GIORNO®
    Spinach Fettuccine, cooked, drained

HEAT oil in skillet on medium-high heat. Add chicken and pepper; cook and stir 3 minutes.

STIR in sauce. Cook on medium heat 3 to 5 minutes or until chicken is cooked through. Serve over hot fettuccine. Top with DI GIORNO® Shredded Parmesan Cheese, if desired.   *Makes 3 to 4 servings*

Turkey Bolognese Sauce

½ cup chopped onion
½ cup chopped carrots
½ cup chopped celery
¼ cup chopped green bell pepper
2 ounces Canadian bacon, chopped
2 cloves garlic, minced
1 tablespoon olive oil
½ pound ground turkey breast
½ cup ⅓-less-salt chicken broth
1 can (10 ounces) no-salt-added whole
      tomatoes, undrained
¼ cup no-salt-added tomato paste
1 bay leaf
¼ teaspoon grated nutmeg
⅛ teaspoon ground black pepper
½ pound fresh mushrooms, sliced
½ cup 1% low fat milk

1. Place onion, carrots, celery, bell pepper, bacon and garlic in large saucepan. Add oil; cook and stir over medium heat 5 minutes or until vegetables are tender.

2. Add turkey; cook and stir until completely browned. Add broth, tomatoes, tomato paste, bay leaf, nutmeg and black pepper. Bring to a boil over high heat; cover and reduce heat to medium. Simmer 45 minutes, stirring occasionally. Uncover; simmer 15 minutes.

3. Add mushrooms; simmer 10 minutes. Stir in milk; simmer 5 minutes. Remove bay leaf before serving.

Makes 8 servings

Seafarers' Supper

12 ounces dried CONTADINA® Dalla Casa
     Buitoni Linguine, cooked, drained
     and kept warm
 1 tablespoon olive or vegetable oil
 1 cup (1 large) chopped green bell pepper
 ½ cup chopped onion
1¾ cups (14.5-ounce can) CONTADINA®
     Dalla Casa Buitoni Recipe Ready
     Diced Tomatoes, undrained
 1 cup chicken broth
 ⅔ cup (6-ounce can) CONTADINA® Dalla
     Casa Buitoni Italian Paste with
     Roasted Garlic
 1 teaspoon Italian herb seasoning
 ¾ teaspoon salt
 ¼ teaspoon ground black pepper
 1 pound orange roughy, cut into 1-inch
     pieces
     Chopped fresh Italian parsley (optional)

HEAT oil in large skillet over medium-high heat. Add
bell pepper and onion; cook for 3 to 4 minutes or until
tender. Stir in tomatoes and juice, broth, tomato paste,
Italian herb seasoning, salt and pepper; bring to a boil.
Reduce heat to low; cook for 5 minutes. Add fish; cook
for 5 minutes or until fish flakes easily when tested
with fork.

SPOON over pasta. Sprinkle with parsley.

Makes 4 to 6 servings

StarKist® Garden Albacore Sauce

- 2 cups chicken broth
- 1 package (1.8 ounces) white sauce mix
- 1 cup shredded Swiss cheese
- 1 can (6 ounces) STARKIST® Solid White Tuna, drained and chunked
- 1 cup sliced mushrooms
- 1 cup sliced bell pepper, green, red and/or yellow
- 1 cup sliced green beans, blanched
- ½ teaspoon seasoned pepper blend
  Hot cooked pasta or rice

In 1½-quart saucepan, combine chicken broth and white sauce mix; blend with wire whisk. Cook over medium-high heat, whisking constantly, until sauce thickens. Reduce heat to low; add Swiss cheese, stirring until melted. Add tuna, mushrooms, bell peppers, green beans and pepper blend; heat thoroughly. Serve over pasta.   *Makes 4 servings*

Seafood Sauce for Pasta

1 tablespoon vegetable oil
1 small green bell pepper, coarsely
    chopped
1 small onion, coarsely chopped
1 clove garlic, minced
2 medium tomatoes, peeled, coarsely
    chopped
1 cup HEINZ® Seafood Cocktail Sauce
½ cup bottled clam juice
½ teaspoon dried basil leaves, crushed
¼ teaspoon dried thyme leaves
¼ teaspoon black pepper
1 pound scallops, peeled and deveined
    shrimp or cubed fish
   Linguine or fettuccine, cooked, drained,
    kept warm

In medium saucepan, heat oil over medium-high heat.
Add bell pepper, onion and garlic; cook and stir until
vegetables are crisp-tender. Add tomatoes, Seafood
Cocktail Sauce, clam juice, basil, thyme and black
pepper. Reduce heat to low; simmer, uncovered, 15
minutes, stirring occasionally. Add scallops; cook 3 to 4
minutes or until scallops are opaque. Serve over pasta.

Makes about 4½ cups sauce

Mushroom-Clam Sauce

½ cup chopped onion
3 cloves garlic, minced
1 tablespoon olive oil, divided
1 pint shucked fresh clams, drained and chopped
1 bottle (8 ounces) clam juice
2 tablespoons lemon juice
½ cup chopped fresh parsley
½ teaspoon dried marjoram leaves
⅛ teaspoon ground black pepper
¼ pound portabella mushrooms, sliced
½ cup dry white wine
2 teaspoons cornstarch

1. Place onion, garlic and 1 teaspoon oil in heavy large saucepan. Cook and stir over medium heat 3 minutes or until onion is tender. Stir in clams, clam juice, lemon juice, parsley, marjoram and black pepper. Bring to a boil; reduce heat. Simmer, uncovered, 10 minutes or until clams are tender.

2. Combine mushrooms and remaining 2 teaspoons oil in small saucepan. Cook and stir until mushrooms are tender. Set aside.

3. Blend wine and cornstarch in small bowl until smooth. Add to clam mixture; mix well. Simmer 1 minute or until thickened. Mix in mushrooms just before serving.   *Makes 8 (¼-cup) servings*

Spicy Pasta Del Mar

- 1 medium onion, diced
- 1 teaspoon olive oil
- 1 (10-ounce) can baby clams, drained
- 2 teaspoons minced garlic
- 1 (26-ounce) jar HEALTHY CHOICE® Traditional Pasta Sauce
- 1 teaspoon dried basil
- ½ teaspoon dried thyme
- ⅛ teaspoon black pepper
- ⅛ teaspoon cayenne pepper
- ½ pound raw medium shrimp, peeled and deveined
- ½ pound linguine, cooked and drained

In large saucepan, sauté onion in hot oil until tender. Add clams and garlic; cook and stir 1 minute longer. Stir in pasta sauce, basil, thyme, black pepper and cayenne pepper. Heat, stirring occasionally, until mixture comes to a boil. Add shrimp; reduce heat to medium; cook until shrimp are pink and cooked through. Serve sauce over linguine.

Makes 6 servings

Primavera Sauce with Artichoke Hearts and Shrimp

- 2 tablespoons olive oil
- 1 cup (1 large) chopped carrot
- 1 cup (2 large stalks) chopped celery
- 1 cup (1 small) chopped onion
- 3 cloves garlic, finely chopped
- 3½ cups (28-ounce can) CONTADINA® Dalla Casa Buitoni Seasoned Crushed Tomatoes with Italian Herbs
- ½ teaspoon salt
- ¼ teaspoon ground black pepper
- 8 ounces medium uncooked shrimp, peeled, deveined
- 1 cup sliced artichoke hearts
  Fresh chopped basil (optional)
  Hot cooked pasta or rice (optional)

HEAT oil in large skillet over high heat. Add carrots, celery, onion and garlic. Cook for 4 to 5 minutes or until carrots are crisp-tender.

ADD tomatoes, salt and pepper. Bring to a boil. Add shrimp and artichoke hearts; cook for 2 to 3 minutes or until shrimp turn pink. Reduce heat to low; cook for 2 minutes or until flavors are blended.

SPRINKLE with basil. Serve over pasta.

Makes 6 servings

Garlic Pesto Sauce

 4 **cups tightly packed fresh spinach leaves**
 2 **tablespoons olive oil**
 3 **tablespoons toasted pine nuts**
 1 **teaspoon sugar**
1½ **teaspoons lemon juice**
 ¾ **teaspoon LAWRY'S® Seasoned Salt**
 ½ **teaspoon LAWRY'S® Garlic Pepper**
    Seasoning
 ¼ **cup grated Parmesan cheese**
 8 **ounces fettuccine pasta, cooked and**
    drained

In food processor, combine spinach, oil, 2 tablespoons pine nuts, sugar, lemon juice, Seasoned Salt and Garlic Pepper. Process 2 minutes until smooth; stir in Parmesan cheese.   *Makes 1½ cups*

Presentation: Toss with fettuccine, sprinkle with remaining 1 tablespoon pine nuts and additional Parmesan cheese.

Linguine with Spinach Pesto

1 (10-ounce) package frozen chopped
　　spinach, thawed and well drained
1 cup EGG BEATERS® Healthy Real Egg
　　Product
⅓ cup PLANTER'S® Walnut Pieces
¼ cup grated Parmesan cheese
2 cloves garlic, crushed
1 pound thin linguine, cooked in unsalted
　　water and drained
½ cup diced red bell pepper
　　Additional grated Parmesan cheese,
　　optional

In electric blender container or food processor, blend
spinach, Egg Beaters®, walnuts, ¼ cup cheese and
garlic until smooth. Toss with hot linguine and bell
pepper. Top with additional cheese, if desired.

Makes 8 servings

Sweet Peppered Pasta

3 tablespoons MAZOLA® Corn Oil
½ cup finely chopped onion
½ cup minced red bell pepper
½ cup minced yellow bell pepper
3 large cloves garlic, minced
⅓ cup water
2 tablespoons chopped fresh basil
1 chicken-flavor bouillon cube
¼ teaspoon crushed red pepper
7 ounces MUELLER'S® Pasta Ruffles
   (about 2⅗ cups), hot cooked and
   drained
   Salad greens, optional

1. In large skillet, heat corn oil over medium-high heat. Add onion, red and yellow bell peppers and garlic; cook and stir 4 minutes.

2. Stir in water, basil, bouillon cube and crushed red pepper. Bring to a boil, stirring occasionally. Reduce heat to low; simmer 4 minutes.

3. Spoon over pasta in large bowl; toss to coat well. Serve on assorted salad greens, if desired.

Makes 6 servings

Italian Garden Fusilli

1   package (8 ounces) dried fusilli pasta,
      cooked, drained and kept warm
1¾ cups (14.5-ounce can) CONTADINA®
      Dalla Casa Buitoni Recipe Ready
      Diced Tomatoes, undrained
1   cup (4 ounces) fresh green beans, cut
      into 2-inch pieces
½   teaspoon garlic salt
¼   teaspoon dried rosemary, crushed
1   cup (1 large) thinly sliced zucchini
¾   cup (1 small) thinly sliced yellow
      squash
1½ cups (*two* 6-ounce jars) marinated
      artichoke hearts, undrained
1   cup frozen peas, thawed
½   teaspoon salt
¼   teaspoon ground black pepper
¼   cup (1 ounce) grated Parmesan cheese

COMBINE tomatoes and juice, beans, garlic salt and rosemary in large skillet. Bring to a boil. Reduce heat to low; cook, covered, for 3 minutes.

ADD zucchini and squash; cover. Cook for 3 minutes or until vegetables are tender. Stir in artichoke hearts and marinade, peas, salt and pepper; heat through.

TOSS vegetables with pasta; sprinkle with cheese.

Makes 6 to 8 servings

Broccoli and Cauliflower Linguine

2   packages (8 ounces *each*) dried
        CONTADINA® Dalla Casa Buitoni
        Linguine, cooked, drained and kept
        warm
2   tablespoons olive oil
2   cups (1 medium bunch) broccoli
        flowerets
2   cups (1 medium bunch) cauliflower
        flowerets
3   cloves garlic, finely chopped
3½ cups (*two* 14.5-ounce cans)
        CONTADINA® Dalla Casa Buitoni
        Pasta Ready Chunky Tomatoes with
        Olive Oil, Garlic & Spices, undrained
1   teaspoon salt
¼   teaspoon crushed red pepper
½   cup dry sherry wine
½   cup (2 ounces) grated Romano cheese
½   cup finely chopped fresh cilantro

HEAT oil in large skillet over medium-high heat. Add broccoli, cauliflower and garlic; cook for 3 minutes. Add tomatoes and juice, salt and crushed red pepper; bring to a boil. Reduce heat to low; cook, stirring occasionally, for 20 minutes.

ADD sherry; cook for 3 minutes. Toss vegetable mixture, pasta, cheese and cilantro together in large bowl.   *Makes 8 servings*

Four-Pepper Penne

- 1 medium onion, sliced
- 1 small red bell pepper, thinly sliced
- 1 small green bell pepper, thinly sliced
- 1 small yellow bell pepper, thinly sliced
- 1½ teaspoons minced garlic
- 1 tablespoon vegetable oil
- 1 (26-ounce) jar HEALTHY CHOICE® Traditional Pasta Sauce
- 1 teaspoon dried basil
- ½ teaspoon dried savory
- ¼ teaspoon black pepper
- ½ pound penne, cooked and drained

In Dutch oven or large nonstick saucepan, cook and stir onion, bell peppers and garlic in hot oil until vegetables are tender-crisp. Add pasta sauce, basil, savory and black pepper. Heat through over medium heat. Serve over penne.   *Makes 6 servings*

Pasta with Roasted Vegetables

1   (2-pound) butternut squash, peeled,
    seeded and cut into 1-inch cubes
1   (10-ounce) container fresh Brussels
    sprouts, each cut in half
1   small bulb fennel (about 8 ounces),
    trimmed, halved and thinly sliced
3   large cloves garlic, peeled and halved
    lengthwise
¼   cup olive oil
¾   teaspoon salt
½   teaspoon dried oregano leaves
1   (8-ounce) box penne or ziti pasta
¼   cup pumpkin seeds
1½ teaspoons TABASCO® pepper sauce
½   cup grated Parmesan cheese

• Preheat oven to 450°F. In a roasting pan, combine
squash chunks, Brussels sprouts, fennel, garlic, olive
oil, salt and oregano. Bake 20 minutes, stirring
occasionally.

• Meanwhile, prepare penne or ziti as package label
directs. During last 2 minutes of roasting vegetables,
add pumpkin seeds to the vegetables. Continue
cooking until seeds are lightly toasted.

• To serve, toss cooked, drained pasta with roasted
vegetables, TABASCO® sauce and Parmesan cheese to
mix well.   *Makes 4 servings*

Pasta Primavera with Roasted Garlic Sauce

3 large heads garlic
2 tablespoons margarine, melted
3 tablespoons GREY POUPON®
    COUNTRY DIJON® Mustard
3 tablespoons lemon juice
¼ teaspoon coarsely ground black pepper
1 cup sliced fresh mushrooms
½ cup julienned zucchini
½ cup julienned carrot
½ cup COLLEGE INN® Lower Sodium
    Chicken Broth or water
1 cup chopped tomato
1 tablespoon chopped fresh basil leaves *or*
    1 teaspoon dried basil leaves
8 ounces angel hair pasta, cooked and
    drained

Brush each head of garlic lightly with 1 teaspoon melted margarine; wrap each head separately in foil. Place in small baking pan; bake at 400°F for 45 minutes or until tender. Cool 10 minutes. Separate cloves; squeeze cloves to extract pulp (discard skins).

In electric blender or food processor, purée garlic pulp, mustard, lemon juice and pepper; set aside.

In skillet, over medium-high heat, sauté mushrooms, zucchini and carrot in remaining spread until tender-crisp, about 3 minutes; add garlic mixture, broth or water, tomato and basil. Reduce heat to low; cook and stir until sauce is heated through. Toss with hot cooked pasta. Serve immediately.

Makes 4 servings

Pasta Ratatouille

1 **medium onion, halved and thinly sliced**
2 **cloves garlic, minced**
2 **tablespoons vegetable oil**
1 **small eggplant (1 pound), peeled, cut into ½-inch cubes**
2 **medium zucchini, halved lengthwise, cut into ¼-inch slices**
2 **cans (16 ounces each) tomatoes, undrained, cut into bite-size pieces**
¼ **cup HEINZ® Worcestershire Sauce**
1½ **teaspoons Italian seasoning**
¼ **teaspoon pepper**
8 **ounces uncooked linguine**
½ **cup grated Parmesan cheese**
   Additional Parmesan cheese, optional

In large skillet, cook and stir onion and garlic in oil until onion is tender. Stir in eggplant, zucchini, tomatoes with juice, Worcestershire sauce, Italian seasoning and pepper. Simmer, covered, 20 minutes, stirring occasionally. Meanwhile, cook linguine according to package directions; drain. In large bowl, toss linguine with vegetable mixture and ½ cup Parmesan cheese. Serve with additional Parmesan cheese, if desired.

Makes 4 to 6 servings

Pasta with Spinach-Cheese Sauce

¼ cup FILIPPO BERIO® Extra-Virgin
    Flavorful Olive Oil, divided
1 medium onion, chopped
1 clove garlic, chopped
3 cups chopped fresh spinach, washed
    and well drained
1 cup lowfat ricotta or cottage cheese
½ cup chopped fresh parsley
1 teaspoon dried basil leaves, crushed
1 teaspoon lemon juice
¼ teaspoon black pepper
¼ teaspoon ground nutmeg
¾ pound uncooked spaghetti

1. Heat 3 tablespoons olive oil in large skillet over medium heat. Cook and stir onion and garlic until onion is tender.

2. Add spinach to skillet; cook 3 to 5 minutes or until spinach wilts.

3. Place spinach mixture, cheese, parsley, basil, lemon juice, pepper and nutmeg in covered blender container. Blend until smooth. Leave in blender, covered, to keep sauce warm.

4. Cook pasta according to package directions. Do not overcook. Drain pasta, reserving ¼ cup water. In large bowl, toss pasta with remaining 1 tablespoon olive oil.

5. Add reserved ¼ cup water to sauce in blender. Blend; serve over pasta. *Makes 4 servings*

Southwestern Pasta Sauce

¼ cup olive oil
2 medium onions, sliced
1 clove garlic, minced
3½ cups canned tomatoes, crushed or
   coarsely chopped
¾ teaspoon TABASCO® pepper sauce
¼ teaspoon salt
2 tablespoons fresh cilantro, minced
¼ teaspoon granulated sugar
12 ounces angel hair pasta, freshly cooked
   Grated Parmesan cheese

• Heat oil over medium heat in large, heavy non-aluminum saucepan. Stir in onions and garlic; sauté 10 to 12 minutes or until tender, stirring occasionally. Add tomatoes, TABASCO® sauce, salt, cilantro and sugar; bring to a boil. Reduce heat to low; simmer, uncovered, 30 minutes or until slightly thickened.

• Place hot cooked pasta on heated serving platter; top with sauce. Sprinkle with Parmesan cheese.

Makes 4 servings

Penne with Fresh Herb Tomato Sauce

    1   pound uncooked penne pasta
    4   ripe large tomatoes, peeled and seeded*
    ½   cup tomato sauce
    ¼   cup FILIPPO BERIO® Olive Oil
    1   to 2 tablespoons lemon juice
    2   teaspoons minced fresh parsley *or*
            1 teaspoon dried parsley
    1   teaspoon minced fresh rosemary,
            oregano or thyme *or* 1 teaspoon dried
            Italian seasoning
        Salt and freshly ground black pepper
        Shavings of Parmesan cheese

Cook pasta according to package directions until
al dente (tender but still firm). Drain; transfer to large
bowl. Process tomatoes in blender container or food
processor until smooth. Add tomato sauce. While
machine is running, very slowly add olive oil. Add
lemon juice, parsley and herbs. Process briefly at high
speed. Spoon sauce over hot or room temperature
pasta. Season to taste with salt and pepper. Top with
cheese.   *Makes 4 servings*

*For chunkier sauce, reserve 1 peeled, seeded tomato. Finely chop;
stir into sauce.

Asian Chili Pepper Linguine

1 (12-ounce) package PASTA LABELLA®
   Chili Pepper Linguine
¼ cup vegetable oil
1 small carrot, julienned
1 small yellow squash, julienned
1 medium Spanish onion, chopped
2 cloves crushed garlic
2 tablespoons roasted sesame seeds
2 tablespoons soy sauce

Cook pasta according to package directions. In large
skillet, heat oil. Add carrot, squash, onion and garlic;
sauté for 4 minutes. Add sesame seeds and soy sauce;
simmer for 2 minutes. Season with salt and pepper to
taste. Serve over hot chili pepper linguine.

Makes 3 dinner or 6 appetizer portions

Thai Peanut Noodle Stir-Fry

1 cup COLLEGE INN® Chicken Broth or
   Lower Sodium Chicken Broth
½ cup GREY POUPON® Dijon Mustard
⅓ cup creamy peanut butter
3 tablespoons firmly packed light brown
   sugar
2 tablespoons soy sauce
1 clove garlic, crushed
½ teaspoon minced fresh ginger
1 tablespoon cornstarch
4 cups cut-up vegetables (red pepper,
   carrot, mushrooms, green onions,
   pea pods)
1 tablespoon vegetable oil
1 pound linguine, cooked
   Chopped peanuts and scallion brushes
   for garnish

In medium saucepan, combine chicken broth,
mustard, peanut butter, sugar, soy sauce, garlic, ginger
and cornstarch. Cook over medium heat until mixture
thickens and begins to boil; reduce heat and keep
warm.

In large skillet, over medium-high heat, sauté
vegetables in oil until tender, about 5 minutes. In large
serving bowl, combine hot cooked pasta, vegetables
and peanut sauce, tossing until well coated. Garnish
with chopped peanuts and scallion brushes. Serve
immediately. *Makes 4 to 6 servings*

Peperonata

3   tablespoons olive oil

3   cups (2 medium) thinly sliced red or yellow onions

6   cups (6 medium) thinly sliced red, yellow and green bell peppers

2   large cloves garlic, finely chopped

3½   cups (*two* 14.5-ounce cans) CONTADINA® Dalla Casa Buitoni Recipe Ready Diced Tomatoes, undrained

2   tablespoons chopped fresh parsley *or* 2 teaspoons dried parsley, crushed

1½   tablespoons balsamic or red wine vinegar

1   teaspoon salt

½   teaspoon dried thyme, crushed

¼   teaspoon ground black pepper

HEAT oil in large skillet over medium heat. Add onions; cook for 2 to 3 minutes or until tender. Add bell peppers and garlic; cook, covered, for 5 to 6 minutes or until bell peppers are tender.

STIR in tomatoes and juice, parsley, vinegar, salt, thyme and pepper. Bring to a boil. Reduce heat to low; cook, uncovered, for 12 to 15 minutes or until flavors are blended.

SERVE hot over pasta, broiled chicken, fish or pork, or serve at room temperature on pizza crust or toasted Italian bread slices.   *Makes 4 servings*

Fresh Herb Sauce

1 **cup whipping cream**
¼ **cup HOLLAND HOUSE® Vermouth Cooking Wine**
3 **green onions, chopped**
1 **garlic clove, crushed**
2 **teaspoons chopped fresh basil**
1 **teaspoon chopped fresh thyme**

Bring whipping cream and cooking wine to a boil in a small saucepan. Reduce heat; simmer 10 minutes. Add remaining ingredients; simmer 5 minutes or until slightly thickened. *Makes 1⅓ cups*

Tomato-Sage Sauce

2 **cans (10 ounces each) no-salt-added whole tomatoes, undrained**
1 **teaspoon olive oil**
3 **cloves garlic, minced**
¼ **cup chopped fresh parsley**
2 **tablespoons chopped fresh sage**
2 **teaspoons sugar**
¼ **teaspoon ground black pepper**

1. Place tomatoes in food processor or blender; process until finely chopped. Set aside.

2. Heat oil in medium saucepan over low heat. Add tomatoes, garlic, parsley, sage, sugar and black pepper. Cook over medium heat 30 minutes or until thickened. *Makes 8 (¼-cup) servings*

Garden Vegetable Sauce for Pasta

2 tablespoons vegetable oil
1 clove garlic, minced
2 medium zucchini, cut into bite-sized
   pieces (about 3½ cups)
1½ cups sliced fresh mushrooms
2 medium tomatoes, coarsely chopped
1 cup HEINZ® Chili Sauce
2 tablespoons chopped fresh parsley
½ teaspoon dried oregano leaves
¼ teaspoon dried basil leaves
¼ teaspoon salt
   Dash pepper
   Linguine or spaghetti, cooked, drained,
   kept warm
   Grated Parmesan cheese

In large skillet, heat oil over medium-high heat. Add
garlic; cook and stir 1 to 2 minutes or until lightly
browned. Add zucchini and mushrooms; cook and stir
4 to 5 minutes or until vegetables are tender. Stir in
tomatoes, Chili Sauce, parsley, oregano, basil, salt and
pepper. Reduce heat to low; simmer, uncovered, 10 to
15 minutes or until sauce is desired consistency,
stirring occasionally. Serve over pasta; sprinkle with
Parmesan cheese.   *Makes about 4 cups sauce*

Bell Pepper and Mushroom Pasta Sauce

1   tablespoon WESSON® Vegetable Oil
2   cups julienne-cut green bell peppers
1   cup chopped onion
1   teaspoon minced fresh garlic
1   can (15 ounces) HUNT'S® Tomato
    Sauce
1   can (14½ ounces) HUNT'S® Whole
    Tomatoes, cut up, undrained
1   can (4 ounces) sliced mushrooms,
    drained
1   teaspoon crushed basil leaves
½   teaspoon crushed oregano leaves
¼   teaspoon black pepper
2   tablespoons grated Parmesan cheese
4   cups mostaccioli, cooked and drained

In medium saucepan, heat oil over medium-high heat. Add green peppers, onion and garlic; cook and stir until crisp-tender. Add all remaining ingredients except Parmesan cheese and mostaccioli. Reduce heat to medium-low. Simmer, uncovered, 20 minutes; stirring occasionally. Stir in Parmesan cheese; serve over hot mostaccioli.   *Makes 4 to 6 servings*

Red Pepper & White Bean Pasta Sauce

12 ounces uncooked penne or ziti pasta
 1 teaspoon olive oil
 3 cloves garlic, chopped
 1 jar (11.5 ounces) GUILTLESS
    GOURMET® Roasted Red Pepper
    Salsa
 ¾ cup canned cannellini beans (white
    kidney beans), rinsed well
 ½ cup low sodium chicken or vegetable
    broth, defatted
 ⅓ cup chopped fresh cilantro
 ¼ cup crumbled feta cheese
    Fresh thyme sprigs (optional)

Cook pasta according to package directions. Drain and
keep warm.

Meanwhile, heat oil in medium nonstick skillet over
medium-high heat until hot. Add garlic; cook and stir
30 seconds or until softened. *Do not brown.* Add salsa,
beans, broth and cilantro; bring just to a boil, stirring
occasionally. (If mixture appears too thick, add water,
1 tablespoon at a time, to desired consistency.) To serve,
place pasta in large serving bowl. Add salsa mixture;
toss to coat well. Sprinkle with feta cheese. Garnish
with thyme, if desired.   *Makes 4 servings*

Fresh Tomato, Basil and Ricotta Sauce

3 cups chopped ripe tomatoes
½ cup chopped fresh basil
2 tablespoons minced red onion
1 clove garlic, chopped
1 cup ricotta cheese
¼ cup FILIPPO BERIO® Olive Oil
   Salt and pepper
1 pound pasta, such as rotelle, fusilli, ziti, penne or tubetti, cooked according to package directions, drained, kept warm

Combine tomatoes, basil, onion and garlic in large bowl. Stir in ricotta cheese, olive oil, salt and pepper to taste. Add pasta; toss well. Serve immediately.

Makes 3 cups sauce

Summer Spaghetti

1 pound firm ripe fresh plum tomatoes
1 medium onion
6 pitted green olives
2 medium cloves garlic
⅓ cup chopped fresh parsley
2 tablespoons finely shredded fresh basil
    or ¾ teaspoon dried basil, crumbled
2 teaspoons drained capers
½ teaspoon paprika
¼ teaspoon dried oregano, crumbled
1 tablespoon red wine vinegar
½ cup olive oil
1 pound uncooked spaghetti

1. Chop tomatoes coarsely. Chop onion and olives.
Mince garlic. Combine tomatoes, onion, olives, garlic,
parsley, basil, capers, paprika and oregano in medium
bowl; toss well. Drizzle vinegar over tomato mixture.
Then pour oil over tomato mixture. Stir until
thoroughly mixed. Refrigerate, covered, at least
6 hours or overnight.

2. Just before serving, cook spaghetti in large kettle of
boiling salted water just until al dente, 8 to 12
minutes; drain well. Immediately toss hot pasta with
cold marinated tomato sauce. Serve at once.

Makes 4 to 6 servings

Light

DISHES

Jamaican Seafood Salad

6 ounces uncooked vermicelli noodles
6 ounces fresh or imitation crabmeat
4 ounces cooked medium shrimp
1 cup diagonally sliced yellow squash
1 cup diagonally sliced zucchini
1 tablespoon rice wine vinegar
1 tablespoon reduced sodium soy sauce
1 tablespoon minced fresh cilantro
1 tablespoon fresh lime juice
2 teaspoons Oriental sesame oil
2 teaspoons grated fresh ginger
1 teaspoon lime peel
⅛ teaspoon ground cinnamon

1. Cook noodles according to package directions, omitting salt. Drain and rinse well under cold water until pasta is cool; drain well.

2. Combine crabmeat, shrimp, yellow squash and zucchini in medium bowl.

3. Combine vinegar, soy sauce, cilantro, lime juice, sesame oil, ginger, lime peel and cinnamon in small bowl; pour over seafood mixture.

4. Toss to coat evenly. Serve over noodles, chilled or at room temperature.   *Makes 6 (1-cup) servings*

Nutrients per Serving:

Total Fat	3 g	Cholesterol	56 mg
Calories	136	Sodium	269 mg
Calories from Fat	15%	Carbohydrate	19 g
Saturated Fat	<1 g	Protein	9 g

Chicken, Tortellini and Roasted Vegetable Salad

- 3 cups whole medium mushrooms
- 2 cups cubed zucchini
- 2 cups cubed eggplant
- ¾ cup red onion wedges (about 1 medium)
  Nonstick olive oil cooking spray
- 1½ packages (9-ounce size) reduced fat cheese tortellini
- 6 cups bite-size pieces leaf lettuce and arugula
- 1 pound boneless skinless chicken breasts, cooked and cut into 1×½-inch pieces
  Sun-Dried Tomato and Basil Vinaigrette (page 127)

1. Heat oven to 425°F. Place mushrooms, zucchini, eggplant and onion in 15×10-inch jelly-roll pan. Spray generously with cooking spray; toss to coat. Bake 20 to 25 minutes or until vegetables are browned. Cool to room temperature.

2. Cook tortellini according to package directions; drain. Cool to room temperature.

3. Combine roasted vegetables, tortellini, lettuce and chicken in large bowl. Drizzle with Sun-Dried Tomato and Basil Vinaigrette; toss to coat. Serve immediately.

Makes 8 servings

Sun-Dried Tomato and Basil Vinaigrette

   4   sun-dried tomato halves, not packed
       in oil
       Hot water
  ½   cup defatted low sodium chicken broth
   2   tablespoons finely chopped fresh basil
       or 2 teaspoons dried basil leaves
   2   tablespoons olive oil
   2   tablespoons lemon juice
   2   tablespoons water
   1   clove garlic, minced
  ¼   teaspoon salt
  ¼   teaspoon pepper

1. Place sun-dried tomatoes in small bowl. Pour hot water over tomatoes to cover. Let stand 10 to 15 minutes or until tomatoes are soft. Drain well; chop tomatoes.

2. In small jar with tight-fitting lid, combine tomatoes and remaining ingredients; shake well. Refrigerate until ready to use; shake before using.

Makes about 1 cup

**Nutrients per Serving
(includes Sun-Dried Tomato and Basil Vinaigrette):**

Total Fat	7 g	Dietary Fiber	3 g
Calories	210	Protein	16 g
Calories from Fat	27%	Calcium	137 mg
Saturated Fat	1 g	Iron	4 mg
Cholesterol	31 mg	Vitamin A	851 RE
Sodium	219 mg	Vitamin C	53 mg
Carbohydrate	24 g		

Dietary Exchanges: 1 Starch/Bread, 1½ Lean Meat, 1½ Vegetable, ½ Fat

Smoked Turkey Pasta Salad

8   ounces uncooked ditalini pasta (small
       tubes)
6   ounces smoked turkey or chicken
       breast, skin removed, cut into strips
1   can (15 ounces) light kidney beans,
       drained and rinsed
½   cup thinly sliced celery
¼   cup chopped red onion
⅓   cup reduced fat mayonnaise
2   tablespoons balsamic vinegar
2   tablespoons chopped fresh chives *or*
       green onion
1   tablespoon chopped fresh tarragon *or*
       1½ teaspoons dried tarragon leaves,
       crushed
1   teaspoon Dijon mustard
1   clove garlic, minced
¼   teaspoon ground black pepper
     Lettuce leaves

1. Cook pasta according to package directions,
omitting salt. Drain and rinse well under cold water
until pasta is cool; drain well.

2. Combine pasta, turkey, beans, celery and onion in
medium bowl. Combine mayonnaise, vinegar, chives,

tarragon, mustard, garlic and pepper in small bowl.
Pour over pasta mixture; toss to coat evenly. Serve on
lettuce leaves, if desired.   *Makes 7 (1-cup) servings*

Nutrients per Serving:

Total Fat	5 g	Cholesterol	12 mg
Calories	233	Sodium	249 mg
Calories from Fat	19%	Carbohydrate	34 g
Saturated Fat	1 g	Protein	13 g

Pasta Pesto Salad

PASTA SALAD

 8 ounces three-color rotini pasta
    (corkscrews)
 3 small bell peppers (1 green, 1 red and
    1 yellow), seeded and cut into thin
    strips
 1 pint cherry tomatoes, stemmed and
    halved (2 cups)
 6 ounces (1 block) ALPINE LACE® Fat
    Free Pasteurized Process Skim Milk
    Cheese Product—For Mozzarella
    Lovers, cut into ½-inch cubes
    (1½ cups)
 1 cup thin carrot circles
 1 cup thin strips red onion
 1 cup slivered fresh basil leaves

SPICY DRESSING

 ½ cup (2 ounces) shredded ALPINE
    LACE® Fat Free Pasteurized Process
    Skim Milk Cheese Product—For
    Parmesan Lovers
 ⅓ cup firmly packed fresh parsley
 ⅓ cup extra virgin olive oil
 ⅓ cup red wine vinegar
 2 large cloves garlic
 1 tablespoon whole-grain Dijon mustard
 ¾ teaspoon freshly ground black pepper
 ½ teaspoon salt

1. To make the Pasta Salad: Cook the pasta according to package directions until al dente. Drain in a colander, rinse under cold water and drain again. Place the pasta in a large shallow pasta bowl and toss with the remaining salad ingredients.

2. To make the Spicy Dressing: In a food processor or blender, process all of the dressing ingredients for 30 seconds or until well blended.

3. Drizzle the dressing on the salad and toss to mix thoroughly. Cover with plastic wrap and refrigerate for 1 hour so that the flavors can blend, or let stand at room temperature for 1 hour.

Makes 12 side-dish servings or 6 main-dish servings

Nutrients per Serving
(1 side-dish serving / 1 cup):

Alpine Lace® Recipe		Traditional Recipe	
Total Fat	7 g	Total Fat	11 g
Calories	173	Calories	208
Calories from Fat	59	Calories from Fat	99
Cholesterol	4 mg	Cholesterol	15 mg

Sweet Dijon Pasta Salad

- **8 ounces tricolor rotini**
- **¾ cup plain nonfat yogurt**
- **¼ cup reduced-fat mayonnaise**
- **2 tablespoons honey**
- **1 tablespoon Dijon mustard**
- **¼ teaspoon cumin**
- **¼ teaspoon salt**
- **1 can (15 ounces) black beans, drained and rinsed**
- **1 medium tomato, chopped**
- **½ cup shredded carrot**
- **¼ cup chopped green onions**

1. Cook pasta according to package directions; drain. Rinse under cold water until cool; drain.

2. Combine yogurt, mayonnaise, honey, mustard, cumin and salt in small bowl until well blended.

3. Combine pasta, beans, tomato, carrot and onions in medium bowl. Add yogurt mixture; toss to coat. Cover and refrigerate until ready to serve. Garnish as desired.

Makes 6 servings

Nutrients per Serving:

Total Fat	1 g	Dietary Fiber	7 g
Calories	237	Protein	12 g
Calories from Fat	4%	Calcium	94 mg
Saturated Fat	<1 g	Iron	1 mg
Cholesterol	1 mg	Vitamin A	293 RE
Sodium	295 mg	Vitamin C	6 mg
Carbohydrate	49 g		

Dietary Exchanges: 3 Starch/Bread, 1 Vegetable

Garden Fresh Macaroni Salad

4	ounces uncooked macaroni pasta
2½	cups chopped seeded tomatoes
1	cup finely chopped red onion
1	cup finely chopped cucumber
½	cup finely chopped celery
½	cup finely chopped green bell pepper
½	cup finely chopped red bell pepper
2	tablespoons finely chopped black olives
3	tablespoons cider vinegar
1	bay leaf
2	tablespoons minced fresh parsley *or* 1 teaspoon dried parsley
1	tablespoon fresh thyme leaves *or* ½ teaspoon dried thyme leaves
1	clove garlic, minced
3	to 4 dashes hot pepper sauce
¼	teaspoon ground black pepper

Cook macaroni according to package directions; omit salt. Drain; rinse well under cold water until cool. Drain. Combine pasta and remaining ingredients in bowl. Cover; refrigerate 4 hours for flavors to blend. Remove bay leaf. Serve chilled or at room temperature.

Makes 6 (1-cup) servings

Nutrients per Serving:

Total Fat	2 g	Cholesterol	0 mg
Calories	136	Sodium	114 mg
Calories from Fat	11%	Carbohydrate	27 g
Saturated Fat	<1 g	Protein	5 g

Nacho Macaroni Soup

¾ cup finely chopped onion
½ cup finely chopped carrot
½ cup finely chopped celery
1 can (14.5 ounces) low sodium chicken
 broth, defatted
2 cups skim milk
1 jar (11.5 ounces) GUILTLESS
 GOURMET® Nacho Dip (mild or
 spicy)
½ cup frozen corn
½ cup frozen peas
1 cup macaroni or small shells, cooked
 according to package directions
 Carrot strips and fresh herbs (optional)

Microwave Directions: Place onion, chopped carrot and
celery in 2-quart glass measure or microwave-safe
casserole. Cover with vented plastic wrap or lid;
microwave on HIGH (100% power) 6 minutes or until
vegetables are tender. Stir in broth, milk and nacho
dip; cover and microwave on HIGH 5 minutes more or
until soup bubbles. Stir in corn and peas; cover and
microwave on HIGH 3 minutes. Stir in warm
macaroni; cover and let stand 3 minutes. To serve,
ladle into 6 individual soup bowls, dividing evenly.
Garnish with carrot strips and fresh herbs, if desired.

Makes 6 servings

Stove Top Directions: Bring 2 tablespoons broth to a
boil in medium nonstick saucepan over medium-high

heat. Add onion, chopped carrot and celery; cook and stir until vegetables are tender. Stir in remaining broth, milk and nacho dip; bring to a boil over medium heat, stirring occasionally. Stir in corn and peas. Reduce heat to low; simmer 10 minutes. Stir in warm macaroni; cover and let stand 3 minutes. Serve as directed.

Nutrients per Serving:

Total Fat	1 g	Sodium	374 mg
Calories	170	Carbohydrate	32 g
Calories from Fat	5%	Dietary Fiber	2 g
Saturated Fat	<1 g	Protein	9 g
Cholesterol	1 mg		

Dietary Exchanges: 1½ Starch/Bread, 1 Vegetable, ⅓ Milk

Minestrone

- 1 tablespoon extra virgin olive oil
- 1 cup chopped red onion
- 2 teaspoons minced garlic
- 5 cups low sodium chicken broth
- 1 cup water
- 1 can (16 ounces) low sodium whole tomatoes, chopped and juices reserved
- 1 bay leaf
- ½ teaspoon salt or to taste
- ¼ teaspoon freshly ground black pepper
- ¾ cup uncooked ditalini pasta (mini macaroni)
- 2 packages (10 ounces each) frozen Italian vegetables
- 1 can (16 ounces) cannellini beans, rinsed and drained
- ⅓ cup slivered fresh basil leaves
- 1 cup (4 ounces) shredded ALPINE LACE® Fat Free Pasteurized Process Skim Milk Cheese Product—For Parmesan Lovers

1. In an 8-quart Dutch oven, heat the oil over medium-high heat. Add the onion and garlic and sauté for 5 minutes or until the onion is soft.

2. Stir in the broth, water, tomatoes and their juices, the bay leaf, salt and pepper. Bring to a rolling boil, add the pasta and return to a rolling boil. Cook, uncovered, for 10 minutes or until the pasta is almost tender.

3. Stir in the vegetables and beans. Return to a boil. Reduce the heat to low and simmer 5 minutes longer or until the vegetables are tender. Remove the bay leaf and discard. Stir in the basil, sprinkle with the cheese and serve immediately.

Makes 10 first-course servings (1 cup each)
or 5 main-dish servings (2 cups each)

Nutrients per Serving (1 cup):

Alpine Lace® Recipe		Traditional Recipe	
Total Fat	2 g	Total Fat	14 g
Calories	167	Calories	324
Calories from Fat	18	Calories from Fat	130
Cholesterol	18 mg	Cholesterol	32 mg

Cheese Tortellini with Tuna

1 tuna steak (about 6 ounces)*
1 package (9 ounces) refrigerated reduced
    fat cheese tortellini
  Nonstick cooking spray
1 cup finely chopped red bell pepper
1 cup finely chopped green bell pepper
¼ cup finely chopped onion
¾ teaspoon fennel seeds, crushed
½ cup evaporated skimmed milk
2 teaspoons all-purpose flour
½ teaspoon dry mustard
½ teaspoon ground black pepper

1. Spray cold grid or broiler rack with nonstick
cooking spray. Grill or broil tuna 4 inches from heat
source until fish just begins to flake, about 7 to
9 minutes, turning once. Remove and discard skin.
Cut tuna into chunks; set aside.

2. Cook pasta according to package directions,
omitting salt. Drain; set aside.

3. Spray large nonstick skillet with cooking spray. Add
bell peppers, onion and fennel seeds; cook over
medium heat until vegetables are crisp-tender.

4. Whisk together milk, flour, mustard and black
pepper in small bowl until smooth; add to skillet. Cook
until thickened, stirring constantly. Stir in tuna and

pasta; reduce heat to low and simmer until heated through, about 3 minutes. Serve immediately.

Makes about 4 (1½-cup) servings

*Or, substitute 1 can (6 ounces) tuna packed in water, drained, for tuna steak. Omit step 1.

Nutrients per Serving:

Total Fat	4 g	Cholesterol	21 mg
Calories	180	Sodium	160 mg
Calories from Fat	19%	Carbohydrate	21 g
Saturated Fat	2 g	Protein	16 g

Shrimp Primavera

8 ounces capelli d'angelo (angel hair pasta), preferably fresh

1½ pounds medium-size fresh shrimp, shelled and deveined, with tails removed

4 teaspoons minced garlic

2 cups thin carrot sticks (about 3 inches long)

2 cups thin strips red bell peppers (about 3 inches long)

2 cups thinly sliced ripe plum tomatoes

2 cups thin strips zucchini (about 3 inches long)

½ teaspoon crushed red pepper flakes

½ cup skim milk

12 ounces (2 cartons) ALPINE LACE® Fat Free Cream Cheese with Garlic & Herbs

1 cup slivered fresh basil leaves *or* 1 cup minced fresh parsley plus 2 tablespoons dried basil
Sprigs of fresh basil (optional)

1. Cook the pasta according to package directions until al dente. Drain, place in a large shallow pasta bowl and keep warm.

2. Fill the same saucepan halfway with water, bring to a boil and cook the shrimp just until pink. Toss with the pasta and keep warm.

3. Spray a large nonstick skillet with nonstick cooking spray and heat over medium-high heat for 1 minute. Add the garlic and sauté for 1 minute. Stir in the carrots, bell peppers, tomatoes, zucchini and red pepper flakes. Cook, stirring constantly, for 5 minutes or until carrots are crisp-tender. Toss with the pasta and shrimp.

4. In a small saucepan, bring the milk to a boil over medium heat. Add the cream cheese and stir until melted. Toss with the pasta mixture, then sprinkle with the basil. Garnish with basil sprigs, if you wish. Serve hot!

Makes 6 servings

Nutrients per Serving (1 cup):

Alpine Lace® Recipe		Traditional Recipe	
Total Fat	3 g	Total Fat	24 g
Calories	288	Calories	433
Calories from Fat	25	Calories from Fat	211
Cholesterol	198 mg	Cholesterol	253 mg

Angel Hair Pasta with Seafood Sauce

½ pound firm whitefish, such as sea bass,
     monkfish or grouper
2 teaspoons olive oil
½ cup chopped onion
2 cloves garlic, minced
3 pounds fresh plum tomatoes, seeded
     and chopped
¼ cup chopped fresh basil
2 tablespoons chopped fresh oregano
1 teaspoon crushed red pepper
½ teaspoon sugar
2 bay leaves
½ pound fresh bay scallops or shucked
     oysters
8 ounces uncooked angel hair pasta
2 tablespoons chopped fresh parsley

1. Cut whitefish into ¾-inch pieces. Set aside.

2. Heat oil in large nonstick skillet over medium heat;
add onion and garlic. Cook and stir 3 minutes or until
onion is tender. Reduce heat to low; add tomatoes,
basil, oregano, crushed red pepper, sugar and bay
leaves. Cook, uncovered, 15 minutes, stirring
occasionally.

3. Add whitefish and scallops. Cook, uncovered, 3 to
4 minutes or until fish flakes easily when tested with
fork and scallops are opaque. Remove bay leaves;
discard. Set seafood sauce aside.

4. Cook pasta according to package directions, omitting salt. Drain well.

5. Combine pasta with seafood sauce in large serving bowl. Mix well. Sprinkle with parsley. Serve immediately. *Makes 6 servings*

Nutrients per Serving:

Total Fat	5 g	Dietary Fiber	5 g
Calories	272	Protein	21 g
Calories from Fat	15%	Calcium	75 mg
Saturated Fat	1 g	Iron	4 mg
Cholesterol	31 mg	Vitamin A	189 RE
Sodium	134 mg	Vitamin C	47 mg
Carbohydrate	38 g		

Dietary Exchanges: 2 Starch/Bread, 1½ Lean Meat, 2 Vegetable

Mac & Cheese with Crunchy Herb Crust

1 pound elbow macaroni
1 cup chopped yellow onion
1 cup chopped red bell pepper
1 cup herb seasoned dry stuffing,
   crumbled, divided
1½ cups skim milk
12 ounces (2 cartons) ALPINE LACE®
   Fat Free Cream Cheese with
   Garlic & Herbs
1 teaspoon low sodium Worcestershire
   sauce
¼ teaspoon ground nutmeg
   Paprika
2 tablespoons extra virgin olive oil

• Preheat the oven to 350°F. Spray a 12-inch round or oval ovenproof baking dish with nonstick cooking spray. Cook the macaroni according to package directions until al dente. Drain well, place in the baking dish and keep warm.

• Spray a large nonstick skillet with the nonstick cooking spray and heat over medium-high heat for 1 minute. Add the onion and bell pepper and sauté for 5 minutes or until soft. Toss with the macaroni and ½ cup of the stuffing.

• In a small saucepan, bring the milk to a boil over medium heat. Add the cream cheese and stir until melted. Remove from the heat and stir in the Worcestershire and nutmeg. Pour over the macaroni mixture. *Do not stir.*

• Top with the remaining ½ cup of stuffing, then sprinkle with the paprika and olive oil. Cover tightly with foil and bake for 30 minutes or until bubbly and hot. Serve hot!

Makes 8 servings

Nutrients per Serving:

Total Fat	4 g	Calories from Fat	36
Calories	195	Cholesterol	8 mg

Noodles Thai Style

¼ cup ketchup
2 tablespoons reduced-sodium soy sauce
1 tablespoon sugar
¼ to ½ teaspoon crushed red pepper
¼ teaspoon ground ginger
2 teaspoons margarine, divided
1 cup EGG BEATERS® Healthy Real Egg
   Product
8 green onions, cut into 1½-inch pieces
1 clove garlic, minced
¾ pound fresh bean sprouts, rinsed and
   well drained
8 ounces linguine, cooked and drained
¼ cup PLANTERS® Dry Roasted Unsalted
   Peanuts, chopped

In bowl, combine ketchup, soy sauce, sugar, pepper and ginger; set aside. In nonstick skillet, over medium heat, melt 1 teaspoon margarine. Pour Egg Beaters® into skillet. Cook; stir occasionally until set. Remove to another bowl. In same skillet, over medium heat, sauté onions and garlic in remaining margarine for 2 minutes. Stir in bean sprouts; cook for 2 minutes. Stir in ketchup mixture; cook until heated. Transfer to bowl; add eggs and linguine. Toss until combined. Top with peanuts. *Makes 6 (1-cup) servings*

Nutrients per Serving:

Total Fat	5 g	Cholesterol	0 mg
Calories	250	Sodium	394 mg
Saturated Fat	1 g	Dietary Fiber	3 g

Spicy Parsley Sauce with Angel Hair Pasta

1 cup chopped fresh parsley
2 fresh red chili peppers, seeded and chopped
  Dash hot red pepper sauce
1 clove garlic, minced
2 tablespoons lemon juice
1 teaspoon grated lemon peel
⅛ teaspoon ground black pepper
4 teaspoons olive oil
¼ cup slivered almonds
1 teaspoon cornstarch
½ cup ⅓-less-salt chicken broth
½ pound uncooked angel hair pasta

1. Combine parsley, chili peppers, hot pepper sauce, garlic, lemon juice, lemon peel and black pepper in medium bowl. Blend well. Mix in oil and almonds.

2. Combine cornstarch and broth in small saucepan. Cook and stir over low heat 3 to 5 minutes or until thickened. Remove from heat; add to parsley mixture.

3. Cook pasta according to package directions; omit salt. Drain well; transfer to bowl. Pour parsley sauce over pasta; mix well.   *Makes 8 servings*

Nutrients per Serving:

Total Fat	5 g	Cholesterol	0 mg
Calories	146	Sodium	11 mg
Calories from Fat	30%	Carbohydrate	21 g
Saturated Fat	1 g	Protein	5 g

Dietary Exchanges: 1 Starch/Bread, 1 Vegetable, 1 Fat

Ravioli with Homemade Tomato Sauce

    3 cloves garlic
    ½ cup fresh basil
    3 cups seeded, peeled tomatoes, cut into
        quarters
    2 tablespoons tomato paste
    2 tablespoons fat-free Italian salad
        dressing
    1 tablespoon balsamic vinegar
    ¼ teaspoon ground black pepper
    1 package (9 ounces) refrigerated
        reduced-fat cheese ravioli
    2 cups shredded spinach leaves
    1 cup (4 ounces) shredded part-skim
        mozzarella cheese

1. To prepare tomato sauce, process garlic in food processor until coarsely chopped. Add basil; process until coarsely chopped. Add tomatoes, tomato paste, salad dressing, vinegar and pepper; process using on/off pulsing action until tomatoes are chopped.

2. Spray 9-inch square microwavable dish with nonstick cooking spray. Spread 1 cup tomato sauce in dish. Layer half of ravioli and spinach over tomato sauce. Repeat layers with 1 cup tomato sauce and remaining ravioli and spinach. Top with remaining 1 cup of tomato sauce.

3. Cover with plastic wrap; refrigerate 1 to 8 hours.
Vent plastic wrap. Microwave at MEDIUM (50%)
20 minutes or until pasta is tender and hot. Sprinkle
with cheese. Microwave at HIGH 3 minutes or just
until cheese melts. Let stand, covered, 5 minutes
before serving.   *Makes 6 servings*

Nutrients per Serving:

Total Fat	6 g	Dietary Fiber	3 g
Calories	206	Protein	13 g
Calories from Fat	26%	Calcium	203 mg
Saturated Fat	3 g	Iron	2 mg
Cholesterol	40 mg	Vitamin A	237 RE
Sodium	401 mg	Vitamin C	28 mg
Carbohydrate	26 g		

Dietary Exchanges: 1 Starch/Bread, 1 Lean Meat, 2 Vegetable, ½ Fat

Spicy Sesame Noodles

6 ounces uncooked dry soba (buckwheat)
   noodles
2 teaspoons sesame oil
1 tablespoon sesame seeds
½ cup ⅓-less-salt chicken broth
1 tablespoon creamy peanut butter
4 teaspoons light soy sauce
½ cup thinly sliced green onions
½ cup minced red bell pepper
1½ teaspoons finely chopped seeded
   jalapeño pepper
1 clove garlic, minced
¼ teaspoon red pepper flakes

1. Cook noodles according to package directions. *Do not overcook.* Rinse noodles thoroughly with cold water to stop cooking and remove salty residue; drain. Place noodles in large bowl; toss with sesame oil.

2. Place sesame seeds in small skillet. Cook over medium heat about 3 minutes or until seeds begin to pop and turn golden brown, stirring frequently. Remove from heat; set aside.

3. Combine chicken broth and peanut butter in small bowl with wire whisk until blended. (Mixture may look curdled.) Stir in soy sauce, green onions, red bell pepper, jalapeño, garlic and red pepper flakes.

4. Pour mixture over noodles; toss to coat. Cover and let stand 30 minutes at room temperature or refrigerate up to 24 hours. Sprinkle with toasted sesame seeds before serving. Garnish, if desired.

Makes 6 servings

Nutrients per Serving:

Total Fat	4 g	Dietary Fiber	1 g
Calories	145	Protein	6 g
Calories from Fat	23%	Calcium	22 mg
Saturated Fat	1 g	Iron	1 mg
Cholesterol	0 mg	Vitamin A	156 RE
Sodium	358 mg	Vitamin C	47 mg
Carbohydrate	24 g		

Dietary Exchanges: 1½ Starch/Bread, ½ Vegetable, ½ Fat

Grilled Ratatouille

3 tablespoons red wine vinegar
1 tablespoon olive oil
2 teaspoons chopped fresh thyme leaves
½ teaspoon ground black pepper
4 small Japanese eggplants, cut
   lengthwise into ½-inch-thick slices
2 small zucchini, cut in half lengthwise
1 medium red onion, cut into quarters
1 red bell pepper, cut into halves and
   seeded
1 yellow bell pepper, cut into halves and
   seeded
6 ounces uncooked ziti or penne pasta
½ cup ⅓-less-salt chicken broth
1 tablespoon honey
1 tablespoon Dijon mustard
½ teaspoon Italian seasoning
¼ teaspoon salt
1 cup cherry tomato halves

1. Combine vinegar, oil, thyme and black pepper in shallow bowl. Add eggplants, zucchini, onion and bell peppers; toss to coat evenly. Let stand at room temperature 1 hour or cover and refrigerate overnight.

2. Cook pasta according to package directions, omitting salt. Drain and rinse well under cold water; set aside.

3. Remove vegetables from marinade; reserve marinade. Grill vegetables over medium-hot coals until tender, about 3 to 4 minutes per side. Cool vegetables;

cut into 1-inch pieces. Combine vegetables and pasta in large bowl. Add broth, honey, mustard, Italian seasoning and salt to reserved vegetable marinade; whisk to combine. Pour over vegetable-pasta mixture; toss to coat evenly. Gently stir in tomatoes. Serve chilled or at room temperature.

Makes 9 (1-cup) servings

Nutrients per Serving:

Total Fat	2 g	Cholesterol	0 mg
Calories	115	Sodium	91 mg
Calories from Fat	18%	Carbohydrate	21 g
Saturated Fat	<1 g	Protein	4 g

Alpine Fettuccine

½ pound white fettuccine, preferably fresh
½ pound green fettuccine, preferably fresh
1½ teaspoons extra virgin olive oil
1 cup sliced fresh mushrooms
1 cup chopped red bell pepper
½ cup skim milk
6 ounces (1 carton) ALPINE LACE®
    Fat Free Cream Cheese with
    Garlic & Herbs

1. Cook the fettuccine according to package directions until al dente. Drain well and place in a large shallow pasta bowl. Toss with the oil and keep warm.

2. Meanwhile, spray a medium-size nonstick skillet with nonstick cooking spray. Add the mushrooms and bell pepper and sauté until soft. Toss with the fettuccine.

3. In a small saucepan, bring the milk to a boil over medium heat. Add the cream cheese and stir until melted. Toss with pasta and serve immediately.

*Makes 9 side-dish servings (1 cup each) or
6 main-dish servings (1½ cups each)*

Nutrients per Serving (1 cup):

Alpine Lace® Recipe		Traditional Recipe	
Total Fat	3 g	Total Fat	15 g
Calories	228	Calories	315
Calories from Fat	26	Calories from Fat	130
Cholesterol	51 mg	Cholesterol	87 mg

Nacho Macaroni

8 ounces uncooked elbow macaroni
1 jar (11.5 ounces) GUILTLESS
    GOURMET® Nacho Dip (mild or
    spicy)
½ cup skim milk
    Nonstick cooking spray
¼ cup (about 20) crushed GUILTLESS
    GOURMET® Baked Tortilla Chips
    (yellow or white corn)

Prepare macaroni according to package directions; drain and keep warm. Preheat oven to 300°F. Combine nacho dip and milk in 4-cup glass measure; microwave on HIGH (100% power) 2 minutes. Pour over cooked macaroni; stir to coat well. Coat 2-quart casserole dish with cooking spray. Add macaroni mixture; top with crushed chips. Bake 20 to 30 minutes or until bubbly and lightly browned on top. Serve hot.

Makes 6 servings

Stove Top Directions: Combine nacho dip and milk in 2-quart saucepan; cook over medium heat, stirring until completely mixed. Add cooked macaroni; stir to coat well. Continue as directed.

Nutrients per Serving:

Total Fat	<1 g	Sodium	330 mg
Calories	220	Carbohydrate	44 g
Calories from Fat	4%	Dietary Fiber	<1 g
Saturated Fat	0 g	Protein	8 g
Cholesterol	0 mg		

Dietary Exchanges: 3 Starch/Bread

Stuffed Manicotti

MANICOTTI
- 12 ounces manicotti (about 12)
- 2 cups (8 ounces) shredded ALPINE LACE® Reduced Sodium Low Moisture Part-Skim Mozzarella Cheese
- 2 cups part-skim ricotta cheese
- ⅓ cup slivered fresh basil leaves *or* 2 tablespoons dried basil
- ¼ cup Italian seasoned dry bread crumbs

PARMESAN SAUCE
- 1½ cups 2% low fat milk
- 2 tablespoons all-purpose flour
- 1 teaspoon Worcestershire sauce
- ¼ teaspoon crushed red pepper flakes
- 1 cup (4 ounces) shredded ALPINE LACE® Fat Free Pasteurized Process Skim Milk Cheese Product—For Parmesan Lovers, divided

1. Preheat the oven to 375°F. Spray a 13×9×2-inch baking dish with nonstick cooking spray. Prepare the manicotti according to package directions; transfer to paper towels and keep warm.

2. To stuff the Manicotti: In a small bowl, stir together the mozzarella cheese, ricotta cheese, basil and bread crumbs. Using a small spoon, stuff the manicotti with the cheese mixture. Arrange in a single layer in the baking dish.

3. To make the Parmesan Sauce: In a medium-size saucepan, combine the milk, flour, Worcestershire and red pepper flakes. Bring to a boil, stirring constantly, over medium-high heat until the sauce thickens. Stir in ½ cup of the Parmesan.

4. Pour the sauce over the manicotti, completely covering the top. Sprinkle with the remaining ½ cup of the Parmesan. Cover with foil and bake for 20 minutes or until bubbly.

5. Uncover the baking dish; turn the oven to broil and broil 4 inches from the heat for 2 minutes or until golden brown.

Makes 12 first-course servings (1 manicotti)
or 6 main-dish servings (2 manicotti)

Nutrients per Serving (1 manicotti):

Alpine Lace® Recipe		Traditional Recipe	
Total Fat	8 g	Total Fat	14 g
Calories	257	Calories	300
Calories from Fat	70	Calories from Fat	121
Cholesterol	37 mg	Cholesterol	46 mg

Family

FAVORITES

Beef with Noodles

- - -

8   ounces Chinese-style thin egg noodles,
        cooked and drained
½   cup water
3   teaspoons soy sauce, divided
¼   teaspoon salt
2   teaspoons instant chicken bouillon
        granules
1   pound beef rump steak, trimmed
6   tablespoons vegetable oil, divided
6   green onions, diagonally sliced
1   piece fresh ginger (about 1 inch
        square), pared and thinly sliced
2   cloves garlic, crushed

1. Place a clean towel over wire cooling racks. Spread
cooked noodles evenly over towel. Let dry about
3 hours.

2. Combine water, 2 teaspoons of the soy sauce, the
salt and bouillon granules in small bowl. Cut beef
across the grain into thin slices, about 2-inches long.

3. Heat 4 tablespoons of the oil in wok or large skillet
over high heat. Add noodles and stir-fry 3 minutes.
Pour water mixture over noodles; toss until noodles are
completely coated, about 2 minutes. Transfer noodles
to serving plate; keep warm.

4. Heat remaining 2 tablespoons oil in wok over high
heat. Add beef, onions, ginger, garlic and remaining
1 teaspoon soy sauce. Stir-fry until beef is cooked
through, about 5 minutes. Spoon meat mixture over
noodles.   *Makes 4 servings*

Sweet & Sour Tortellini

1 **package (7 to 12 ounces) cheese-filled tortellini**
½ **pound boneless tender beef steak (sirloin, rib eye or top loin)**
2 **teaspoons cornstarch**
2 **teaspoons KIKKOMAN® Soy Sauce**
1 **small clove garlic, minced**
½ **cup KIKKOMAN® Sweet & Sour Sauce**
⅓ **cup chicken broth**
1 **tablespoon sugar**
2 **tablespoons dry sherry**
2 **tablespoons vegetable oil, divided**
1 **medium onion, chunked**
1 **small red pepper, chunked**
1 **small green pepper, chunked**

Cook tortellini according to package directions, omitting salt; drain. Cut meat into thin bite-size pieces. Combine cornstarch, soy sauce and garlic in small bowl; stir in meat. Let stand 15 minutes. Meanwhile, combine sweet & sour sauce, chicken broth, sugar and sherry; set aside. Heat 1 tablespoon oil in hot wok or large skillet over high heat. Add meat mixture; stir-fry 1 minute. Remove from wok. Heat remaining 1 tablespoon oil in wok. Add onion and peppers; stir-fry 3 minutes. Add meat mixture, sweet & sour sauce mixture and tortellini. Heat thoroughly, stirring occasionally.   *Makes 4 servings*

Ranch Stroganoff

1½ pounds flank steak or top sirloin steak
2 packages (1 ounce each) HIDDEN
    VALLEY RANCH® Milk Recipe
    Original Ranch® Salad Dressing mix
¼ cup all-purpose flour
¼ cup vegetable oil
¼ cup minced onion
1 clove garlic, minced
½ pound fresh mushrooms, thinly sliced
1½ cups milk
8 ounces wide egg noodles, cooked and
    buttered
1 tablespoon poppy seeds

Cut steak diagonally into 2×½-inch strips; set aside.
Combine salad dressing mix and flour in plastic bag.
Add steak and dredge with flour mixture. Place steak
on platter; reserve extra coating mixture. In large
skillet, heat oil over medium heat until hot. Add onion
and garlic; sauté 1 minute. Add steak and mushrooms
and continue cooking until steak is lightly browned,
4 to 5 minutes. Stir in milk and remaining coating
mixture and continue cooking over low heat, stirring
constantly, until thickened. Serve over noodles tossed
with poppy seeds. *Makes 4 servings*

Fajita Stuffed Shells

¼ cup fresh lime juice
1 clove garlic, minced
½ teaspoon dried oregano leaves
¼ teaspoon ground cumin
1 (6-ounce) boneless lean round or flank
   steak
1 medium green bell pepper, halved and
   seeded
1 medium onion, cut in half
12 uncooked jumbo pasta shells (about
   6 ounces)
½ cup reduced-fat sour cream
2 tablespoons shredded reduced-fat
   Cheddar cheese
1 tablespoon minced fresh cilantro
⅔ cup chunky salsa
2 cups shredded leaf lettuce

1. Combine lime juice, garlic, oregano and cumin in shallow nonmetallic dish. Add steak, bell pepper and onion. Cover and refrigerate 8 hours or overnight.

2. Preheat oven to 350°F. Cook pasta shells according to package directions, omitting salt. Drain and rinse well under cold water; set aside.

3. Grill steak and vegetables over medium-hot coals 3 to 4 minutes per side or until desired doneness; cool slightly. Cut steak into thin slices. Chop vegetables. Place steak slices and vegetables in medium bowl. Stir in sour cream, Cheddar cheese and cilantro. Stuff shells evenly with meat mixture, mounding slightly.

4. Arrange shells in 8-inch baking dish. Pour salsa over filled shells. Cover with foil and bake 15 minutes or until heated through. Divide lettuce evenly among 4 plates; arrange 3 shells on each plate.

Makes 4 servings

30-Minute Chili Mac

1 (1-pound) beef top round steak, cut into ¼-inch-thick strips
½ cup chopped onion
1 tablespoon vegetable oil
1 (16-ounce) can whole tomatoes, undrained, coarsely chopped
½ cup A.1.® ORIGINAL or A.1.® BOLD Steak Sauce
2 tablespoons chili powder
1 cup uncooked elbow macaroni, cooked, drained
1 cup drained canned kidney beans, optional
⅓ cup shredded Cheddar cheese (about 1½ ounces)
¼ cup chopped fresh cilantro

In large skillet, over medium heat, cook steak and onion in oil 8 to 10 minutes, stirring occasionally. Stir in tomatoes with liquid, steak sauce and chili powder. Heat to a boil; reduce heat. Cover; simmer 10 minutes or until steak is tender. Stir in macaroni and beans, if desired. Sprinkle with cheese and cilantro. Serve immediately.

Makes 4 servings

String Pie

- 1 **pound ground beef**
- ½ **cup chopped onion**
- ¼ **cup chopped green pepper**
- 1 **jar (15½ ounces) spaghetti sauce**
- 8 **ounces spaghetti, cooked and drained**
- ⅓ **cup grated Parmesan cheese**
- 2 **eggs, beaten**
- 2 **teaspoons butter**
- 1 **cup cottage cheese**
- ½ **cup (2 ounces) shredded mozzarella cheese**

Preheat oven to 350°F. Cook beef, onion and green pepper in large skillet over medium-high heat until meat is browned. Drain fat. Stir in spaghetti sauce. Combine spaghetti, Parmesan cheese, eggs and butter in large bowl; mix well. Place on bottom of 13×9-inch baking pan. Spread cottage cheese over top; cover with sauce mixture. Sprinkle with mozzarella cheese. Bake until mixture is thoroughly heated and cheese is melted, about 20 minutes.   *Makes 6 to 8 servings*

Favorite recipe from **North Dakota Beef Commission**

Baked Cheesy Rotini

¾ pound lean ground beef
½ cup chopped onion
2 cups cooked rotini, drained
1 (15-ounce) can HUNT'S® Ready
   Tomato Sauce Chunky Italian
¼ cup chopped green bell pepper
¾ teaspoon garlic salt
¼ teaspoon black pepper
1½ cups cubed processed American cheese

Preheat oven to 350°F. In large skillet, brown beef with
onion; drain. Stir in rotini, tomato sauce, bell pepper,
garlic salt and black pepper. Pour beef mixture into
1½-quart casserole. Top with cheese. Bake, covered,
20 minutes or until sauce is bubbly.

Makes 6 servings

Pasta "Pizza"

2   cups corkscrew macaroni, cooked and
      drained
3   eggs, slightly beaten
½   cup milk
½   cup (2 ounces) shredded Wisconsin
      Cheddar cheese
¼   cup finely chopped onion
1   pound lean ground beef
1   can (15 ounces) tomato sauce
1   teaspoon dried basil leaves, crushed
1   teaspoon dried oregano leaves, crushed
½   teaspoon garlic salt
1   medium tomato, thinly sliced
1   green pepper, sliced into rings
1½ cups (6 ounces) shredded Wisconsin
      mozzarella cheese

Combine eggs and milk. Add to hot macaroni; mix
lightly to coat. Stir in Cheddar cheese and onion; mix
well. Spread macaroni mixture onto bottom of well-
buttered 14-inch pizza pan. Bake at 350°F, 25 minutes.
Meanwhile, in large skillet over medium-high heat,
brown meat, stirring occasionally to separate meat;
drain. Stir in tomato sauce, basil, oregano and garlic
salt. Spoon over macaroni crust. Arrange tomato slices
and pepper rings on top. Sprinkle with mozzarella
cheese. Continue baking 15 minutes or until cheese is
bubbly.   *Makes 8 servings*

Favorite recipe from **Wisconsin Milk Marketing Board**

Kids' Taco-Mac

1 **pound ground beef**
1 **package (1.0 ounce) LAWRY'S® Taco Spices & Seasonings**
1 **can (14½ ounces) diced tomatoes, undrained**
1½ **cups water**
8 **ounces uncooked macaroni or small spiral pasta**
½ **cup sliced celery**
1 **egg**
⅓ **cup milk**
1 **package (8½ ounces) corn muffin mix**
½ **cup (2 ounces) shredded Cheddar cheese**

In medium skillet, brown ground beef until crumbly; drain. Blend in Taco Spices & Seasonings, tomatoes, water, macaroni and celery. Bring to a boil. Reduce heat to low; cover. Simmer 20 minutes, stirring occasionally. Spoon meat mixture into 2½-quart casserole dish; set aside. Heat oven to 400°F. In medium bowl, beat egg. Stir in milk. Add muffin mix; stir with fork just until muffin mix is moistened. Spoon half of the batter over meat mixture in dollops. Spoon remaining batter into 6 greased or paper-lined medium-sized muffin cups. Bake casserole and muffins 15 to 20 minutes or until golden. Sprinkle with Cheddar cheese before serving.

Makes 6 to 8 servings

Note: Cool muffins completely. Wrap tightly and freeze for later use, if desired.

Five-Way Cincinnati Chili

1 **pound uncooked spaghetti, broken in half**
1 **pound ground chuck**
2 **cans (10 ounces each) tomatoes with green chilies, undrained**
1 **can (10½ ounces) condensed French onion soup**
1 **can (15 ounces) red kidney beans, drained**
1 **tablespoon chili powder**
1 **teaspoon sugar**
½ **teaspoon salt**
¼ **teaspoon cinnamon**
½ **cup (2 ounces) shredded Cheddar cheese**
½ **cup chopped onion**

1. Cook pasta according to package directions; drain.

2. While pasta is cooking, cook and stir beef in large saucepan over medium-high heat until browned; drain. Return meat to saucepan with tomatoes, soup, beans, 1¼ cups water, chili powder, sugar, salt and cinnamon; bring to a boil. Reduce heat to low. Simmer, uncovered, 10 minutes, stirring occasionally. Serve chili over spaghetti; sprinkle with cheese and onion.

Makes 6 servings

Skillet Spaghetti and Sausage

 ¼ pound mild or hot Italian sausage links,
    sliced
 ½ pound ground beef
 ¼ teaspoon dried oregano, crushed
 4 ounces spaghetti, broken in half
 1 can (26 ounces) DEL MONTE® Chunky
    Spaghetti Sauce with Garlic & Herb
1½ cups sliced fresh mushrooms
 2 stalks celery, sliced

1. Brown sausage in large skillet over medium-high heat. Add beef and oregano; season to taste with salt and pepper, if desired. Cook, stirring occasionally, until beef is browned; drain.

2. Add pasta, 1 cup water, spaghetti sauce, mushrooms and celery. Bring to a boil, stirring occasionally.

3. Reduce heat; cover and simmer 12 to 14 minutes or until spaghetti is tender. Garnish with grated Parmesan cheese and chopped parsley, if desired. Serve immediately.   *Makes 4 to 6 servings*

Vermicelli with Pork

4 ounces Chinese rice vermicelli or bean threads
32 dried mushrooms
1 small red or green hot chili pepper*
3 green onions with tops, divided
2 tablespoons minced fresh ginger
2 tablespoons hot bean sauce
1½ cups chicken broth
1 tablespoon soy sauce
1 tablespoon dry sherry
2 tablespoons vegetable oil
6 ounces lean ground pork
Fresh cilantro leaves and hot red pepper for garnish

1. Place vermicelli and dried mushrooms in separate large bowls; cover each with hot water. Let stand 30 minutes; drain. Cut vermicelli into 4-inch pieces.

2. Squeeze out as much excess water as possible from mushrooms. Cut off and discard mushroom stems; cut caps into thin slices.

3. Cut chili pepper in half; scrape out seeds.

4. Finely chop chili pepper.

5. Cut one onion into 1½-inch slivers; reserve for garnish. Cut remaining two onions into thin slices.

6. Combine ginger and hot bean sauce in small bowl; set aside. Combine chicken broth, soy sauce and sherry in another small bowl; set aside.

7. Heat oil in wok or large skillet over high heat. Add meat; stir-fry until no longer pink, about 2 minutes. Add chili pepper, sliced onions and bean sauce mixture; stir-fry 1 minute.

8. Add chicken broth mixture, vermicelli and mushrooms. Simmer, uncovered, until most of the liquid is absorbed, about 5 minutes. Top with onion slivers. Garnish, if desired.   *Makes 4 servings*

*Hot chili peppers are potent. Wear rubber or plastic gloves when removing seeds or chopping peppers and do not touch your eyes or lips when handling.

Mexican Eye-Opener with Chili Pepper Pasta

1 tablespoon olive oil
2½ ounces chorizo sausage
1 ounce onions, diced
1 ounce bell pepper, diced
1 cup cooked PASTA LABELLA® Chili Pepper Linguine
3 large eggs
1 tablespoon water
1½ ounces Cheddar cheese, grated

Heat olive oil in omelet skillet. Sauté chorizo sausage, onions and bell pepper for 1-2 minutes. Add chili pepper pasta and cook until pasta begins to crackle. Whisk eggs and water in small bowl. Add egg mixture and cook in normal omelet fashion. When pasta is flipped over, sprinkle with Cheddar cheese. Melt cheese and serve.   *Makes 1 serving (1 omelet)*

Skillet Pasta Roma

½ pound Italian sausage, sliced or
    crumbled
1 large onion, coarsely chopped
1 large clove garlic, minced
1 can (26 ounces) DEL MONTE®
    Chunky Spaghetti Sauce with
    Garlic & Herb
1 cup water
8 ounces uncooked rotini or other spiral
    pasta
8 sliced mushrooms, optional
    Grated Parmesan cheese and fresh
    parsley sprigs, optional

1. Brown sausage in large skillet. Add onion and garlic.
Cook until onion is soft; drain.

2. Stir in spaghetti sauce, water and pasta. Cover and
bring to a boil; reduce heat. Simmer, covered, 25 to
30 minutes or until pasta is tender, stirring
occasionally.

3. Stir in mushrooms; simmer 5 minutes. Serve in
skillet garnished with cheese and parsley, if desired.

Makes 4 servings

Fettuccine alla Carbonara

¾ **pound uncooked dry fettuccine or spaghetti**

4 **ounces pancetta (Italian bacon) or lean American bacon, cut into ½-inch-wide strips**

3 **cloves garlic, halved**

¼ **cup dry white wine**

⅓ **cup heavy or whipping cream**

1 **egg**

1 **egg yolk**

⅔ **cup freshly grated Parmesan cheese (about 2 ounces), divided**

Generous dash ground white pepper

Fresh oregano leaves for garnish

1. Cook dry fettuccine in large pot of boiling salted water 6 to 8 minutes just until al dente; remove from heat. Drain well; return to dry pot.

2. Cook and stir pancetta and garlic in large skillet over medium-low heat 4 minutes or until pancetta is light brown. Reserve 2 tablespoons drippings in skillet with pancetta. Discard garlic and remaining drippings.

3. Add wine to pancetta mixture; cook over medium heat 3 minutes or until wine is almost evaporated. Stir in cream; cook and stir 2 minutes. Remove from heat.

4. Whisk egg and egg yolk in top of double boiler. Place top of double boiler over simmering water, adjusting heat to maintain simmer. Whisk ⅓ cup cheese and pepper into egg mixture; cook and stir until sauce thickens slightly.

5. Pour pancetta-cream mixture over fettuccine in pot; toss to coat. Heat over medium-low heat until heated through. Stir in egg-cheese mixture. Toss to coat evenly. Remove from heat. Serve with remaining ⅓ cup cheese. Garnish, if desired.   *Makes 4 servings*

Spicy Ham & Cheese Pasta

  ½   (16-ounce) package corkscrew pasta
  2   tablespoons olive oil
  1   large red pepper, cut into julienne strips
  1   small red onion, diced
  1   large garlic clove, crushed
  8   ounces cooked ham, cut into ½-inch
       cubes
  1   cup ricotta cheese
  3   tablespoons chopped parsley
  1   teaspoon TABASCO® pepper sauce
  ¾   teaspoon salt

Prepare pasta as label directs; drain. Meanwhile, in 10-inch skillet over medium heat, in hot olive oil, cook red pepper, onion and garlic until tender-crisp, about 5 minutes. Add ham cubes; cook 3 minutes longer, stirring occasionally. In large bowl, toss cooked pasta with ham mixture, ricotta cheese, parsley, TABASCO® sauce and salt; mix well.   *Makes 4 servings*

Country Noodles and Ham

1 pound package **PASTA LABELLA®**
     Medium or Extra Wide Egg Noodles
¼ cup olive oil
½ cup yellow onions, diced
12 ounces ham, diced large
1 cup mushrooms, sliced
1 cup frozen peas, thawed
1 tablespoon garlic, chopped
2 cups chicken broth
     Salt and pepper, to taste
3 tablespoons sweet cream butter
⅓ cup grated Parmesan cheese

Cook pasta according to package directions.
Meanwhile, heat olive oil in large pot. Sauté onions
and ham for 3 minutes on high heat. Add mushrooms,
peas and garlic and cook for 6 minutes. Add chicken
broth, salt, pepper and sweet cream butter. Simmer for
3 minutes. Sprinkle with Parmesan cheese and serve.

Serves 3 dinner portions or
6 appetizer portions

Macaroni and Cheese Dijon

1¼ cups milk
12 ounces pasteurized process Cheddar cheese spread, cubed
½ cup GREY POUPON® Dijon Mustard
⅓ cup sliced green onions
6 slices bacon, cooked and crumbled
⅛ teaspoon ground red pepper
12 ounces tricolor rotelle or spiral-shaped pasta, cooked
1 (2.8-ounce) can French fried onion rings

In medium saucepan over low heat, heat milk, cheese and mustard until cheese melts and mixture is smooth. Stir in green onions, bacon and pepper; remove from heat.

In large bowl, combine hot pasta and cheese mixture, tossing until well coated; spoon into greased 2-quart casserole. Cover; bake at 350°F for 15 to 20 minutes. Uncover and stir; top with onion rings. Bake, uncovered, for 5 minutes more. Let stand 10 minutes before serving. Garnish as desired.

Makes 6 servings

Linguine Carbonara

12 ounces uncooked linguine
 6 slices bacon, cut into 1-inch pieces
 1 box (10 ounces) BIRDS EYE® frozen
    Deluxe Baby Whole Carrots
 1 cup BIRDS EYE® frozen Green Peas
 ½ cup milk
 ½ teaspoon dried oregano
 ½ teaspoon garlic powder
 ⅓ cup grated Parmesan cheese

• Cook pasta according to package directions; drain.

• Meanwhile, cook bacon in large skillet until golden brown. Drain bacon, reserving 2 tablespoons drippings in skillet.

• Add vegetables, milk, oregano, garlic powder and bacon; cook and stir over medium heat 5 minutes. Add linguine; heat through. Add cheese; toss to coat. Add salt and pepper to taste.   *Makes 4 to 6 servings*

Spam™ Fettuccine Primavera

- 1 tablespoon butter or margarine
- 2 tablespoons all-purpose flour
- 1½ cups skim milk
- ½ cup low sodium chicken broth
- 1½ teaspoons dried basil leaves
- 12 ounces uncooked fettuccine
- 1 (12-ounce) can SPAM® Lite Luncheon Meat, cut into julienne strips
- 1 (16-ounce) package frozen broccoli, carrot and cauliflower combination, cooked and drained
- ⅔ cup grated Parmesan cheese

In small saucepan, melt butter. Stir in flour. Cook and stir 1 minute. Stir in milk, chicken broth and basil. Bring to a boil, stirring constantly, until thickened; keep warm. In 5-quart saucepan, cook fettuccine according to package directions; drain and return to saucepan. Stir in Spam®, vegetables and sauce. Cook and stir over medium-high heat until thoroughly heated. Stir in Parmesan cheese.

Makes 6 to 8 servings

Lamb and Spinach Manicotti

1 (5-ounce) package manicotti pasta

SAUCE

1½ pounds ground American lamb
1 small onion, chopped
1 (16-ounce) jar prepared spaghetti sauce
½ teaspoon salt
¼ teaspoon black pepper

STUFFING

1 tablespoon butter or margarine
1 large onion, finely chopped
2 cloves garlic, minced
2 (10-ounce) packages frozen chopped
   spinach, thawed and drained
2 eggs, lightly beaten
½ teaspoon salt
1 teaspoon dried oregano leaves
½ teaspoon fresh basil leaves, chopped
1 cup ricotta cheese
1 cup shredded Monterey Jack cheese
½ cup grated Parmesan cheese

Cook pasta according to package directions.

To make sauce, brown lamb and onion. Drain well.
Add spaghetti sauce, salt and pepper. Simmer 15 to
20 minutes.

To make stuffing, melt butter in skillet; add onion and
garlic. Cook, stirring constantly, until onion is
transparent. Add spinach; cook until moisture has
evaporated. Remove from heat. Add eggs, salt, oregano,
basil and ricotta. Stuff pasta. Pour thin layer of sauce

in a large baking dish. Arrange stuffed manicotti on sauce. Top with remaining sauce. Cover with Monterey Jack and Parmesan cheeses.

Bake, uncovered, at 350°F for 25 to 30 minutes, or until bubbly and heated through.

Makes 8 servings

Favorite recipe from **American Lamb Council**

Lamb and Spaghetti Primavera

- ½ **pound lean ground American lamb**
- 2 **tablespoons grated Parmesan cheese**
- ¼ **teaspoon garlic powder**
- 2 **cups meatless spaghetti sauce**
- 1 **small zucchini, halved lengthwise and sliced (1½ cups)**
- 1½ **cups sliced fresh mushrooms**
- 8 **ounces spaghetti or linguine**
- 2 **ounces Asiago cheese, shredded (½ cup)***

In a bowl, combine ground lamb, Parmesan cheese and garlic powder; mix well. Form lamb mixture into 24 (¾-inch) balls. Meanwhile, heat spaghetti sauce in a large saucepan. Add meatballs to sauce; bring to a boil. Reduce heat; cover and simmer 5 minutes. Stir in zucchini and mushrooms; cook 6 to 8 minutes more or until vegetables are tender. Meanwhile, cook pasta according to package directions; drain. Serve spaghetti and meatball mixture over pasta; top with shredded Asiago.

Makes 4 servings

*Grated fresh Parmesan may be substituted.

Favorite recipe from **American Lamb Council**

Pasta with Chicken and Peppers

5 tablespoons FILIPPO BERIO® Extra-
  Virgin Flavorful Olive Oil, divided
1 large boneless chicken breast (1 pound),
  skinned and cut into julienne strips
1 medium onion, chopped
1 medium red bell pepper, cut into
  julienne strips
1 medium green bell pepper, cut into
  julienne strips
1 clove garlic, minced
⅛ teaspoon ground red pepper
2 large tomatoes, chopped
¾ pound uncooked pasta tubes, such
  as penne

1. Heat 2 tablespoons olive oil over medium heat in large skillet. Cook and stir chicken until tender. Remove chicken; set aside.

2. Add 2 tablespoons olive oil to skillet; cook and stir onion and bell peppers until tender.

3. Return chicken to pan; add garlic and ground red pepper. Cook for 3 minutes, stirring constantly.

4. Add tomatoes; simmer for 10 minutes.

5. While chicken mixture is simmering, cook pasta according to package directions; do not overcook. Drain and toss with remaining 1 tablespoon olive oil in large bowl. Serve with sauce. *Makes 4 servings*

Chicken Pesto Mozzarella

6 to 8 ounces linguine or corkscrew pasta
4 half boneless chicken breasts, skinned
1 tablespoon olive oil
1 can (14½ ounces) DEL MONTE®
    FreshCut™ Diced Tomatoes with
    Basil, Garlic & Oregano, undrained
½ medium onion, chopped
⅓ cup sliced ripe olives
4 teaspoons pesto sauce*
¼ cup (1 ounce) shredded mozzarella
    cheese

1. Cook pasta according to package directions; drain.

2. Meanwhile, season chicken with salt and pepper, if desired. In large skillet, brown chicken in hot oil over medium-high heat. Add tomatoes, onion and olives; bring to boil. Cover and cook 8 minutes over medium heat.

3. Remove cover; cook about 8 minutes or until chicken is no longer pink in center.

4. Spread 1 teaspoon pesto over each chicken breast; top with cheese. Cover and cook until cheese is melted. Serve over pasta. Garnish, if desired.

Makes 4 servings

*Pesto sauce is available frozen or refrigerated at the supermarket.

Creamy Chicken Florentine

8 ounces uncooked fusilli
1 box (10 ounces) frozen chopped
   spinach
1 package (8 ounces) cream cheese
½ cup canned chicken broth
½ teaspoon dried Italian seasoning
¼ teaspoon salt
¼ teaspoon black pepper
   Dash hot pepper sauce
1 can (10 ounces) premium chunk white
   chicken in water, drained
1 tablespoon lemon juice

1. Cook pasta according to package directions; drain.

2. While pasta is cooking, remove outer wrapping from spinach, leaving spinach in box. Microwave spinach at HIGH 3 minutes or until thawed. Drain in colander; cool slightly. Squeeze spinach to remove excess moisture. Set aside.

3. Combine cream cheese, broth, Italian seasoning, salt, black pepper and hot pepper sauce in microwavable 2-quart casserole. Cover and microwave at HIGH 2 to 3 minutes; whisk until smooth and blended.

4. Add spinach, chicken and lemon juice. Microwave at HIGH 2 to 3 minutes or until hot, stirring after 1 minute.

5. Combine pasta and spinach mixture in large bowl; toss until blended.   *Makes 4 servings*

Grilled Chicken Pasta Toss

6 boneless, skinless chicken breast halves
   (about 1½ pounds)
1 bottle (12 ounces) LAWRY'S® Herb &
   Garlic Marinade with Lemon Juice,
   divided
3 tablespoons vegetable oil, divided
1½ cups broccoli florets and sliced stems
1 cup Chinese pea pods
1 cup diagonally sliced carrots
1 can (2¼ ounces) sliced pitted ripe
   olives, drained
8 ounces fettuccine or linguine noodles,
   cooked, drained and kept hot

Preheat grill. Pierce chicken pieces several times with
fork. In large resealable plastic bag or shallow glass
dish, place chicken. Add 1 cup Lawry's® Herb & Garlic
Marinade with Lemon Juice; seal bag or cover dish.
Refrigerate at least 30 minutes. Remove chicken from
marinade, reserving marinade. Grill chicken, 5 inches
from heat source, 5 to 7 minutes on each side or until
no longer pink in center, brushing halfway through
cooking time with reserved marinade. Remove chicken
from grill; slice chicken. Cover; set aside. In skillet,
heat 2 tablespoons oil. Add broccoli, pea pods and
carrots; sauté until crisp-tender. In bowl, combine
sautéed vegetables, olives, hot noodles and chicken. In
bowl, combine remaining marinade and remaining
1 tablespoon oil. Add just enough dressing to noodle
mixture to coat; toss well. Serve with any remaining
dressing, if desired.   *Makes 4 to 6 servings*

Chicken Siesta Twist

1   pound rotini pasta
1   teaspoon garlic powder
1   packet taco seasoning, divided
2   to 3 boneless, skinless chicken breasts,
      cubed
½   green or red bell pepper, sliced
1   can (10 ounces) tomatoes with green
      chilies
    Sour cream or low-fat sour cream
    Chopped green onions

Cook pasta as directed on package; drain. Mix garlic
powder and all but 1 teaspoon taco seasoning; toss the
garlic-taco mixture with cubed chicken. Spray medium
skillet with cooking spray; brown the chicken. Add bell
peppers and tomatoes. Cover and simmer 10 to
15 minutes. Drain pasta and toss with remaining taco
seasoning. Place on large serving plate. Top with
chicken mixture, sour cream and chopped green
onions.   *Serves 4 to 5*

Favorite recipe from **North Dakota Wheat Commission**

Manicotti Alla Perdue

2 cups finely chopped cooked PERDUE®
  Chicken or Turkey
1 container (15 ounces) ricotta cheese
1 egg, slightly beaten
1 package (10 ounces) frozen chopped
  spinach, thawed and well drained
¼ cup grated Parmesan cheese
½ teaspoon ground nutmeg
3 cups marinara or spaghetti sauce,
  divided
1 package (8 ounces) manicotti shells,
  cooked
½ to ¾ cup shredded mozzarella cheese

Preheat oven to 350°F. In medium bowl, combine first
6 ingredients. Into 12×9-inch baking pan, spoon a thin
layer of marinara sauce. Fill manicotti shells with
chicken or turkey mixture and arrange over sauce.
Pour remaining sauce on top; sprinkle with
mozzarella. Bake 25 to 30 minutes until hot and
bubbly. *Makes 4 to 6 servings*

Micro-Meatball Rigatoni

1   **package (about 1¼ pounds) PERDUE®
    Fresh Ground Chicken or Turkey**
¾   **cup finely chopped onions**
½   **cup seasoned dry bread crumbs
    Grated Parmesan cheese**
1   **can (6 ounces) tomato paste, divided**
1   **teaspoon dried Italian seasoning**
1   **jar (30 ounces) chunky vegetable
    spaghetti sauce**
8   **ounces small rigatoni, cooked and
    drained**

In medium bowl, mix turkey or chicken, chopped
onions, bread crumbs, ¼ cup grated Parmesan,
3 tablespoons tomato paste and Italian seasoning.
Shape mixture into 12 meatballs. In 10-inch
microwave-safe pie plate, arrange meatballs in a circle;
cover with wax paper. Microwave at HIGH (100%
power) 6 minutes. Rearrange and turn meatballs.
Re-cover and microwave at HIGH 4 to 6 minutes
longer.

Meanwhile, in medium bowl, combine spaghetti sauce
and remaining tomato paste; add cooked meatballs.
Discard juices from pie plate. Place rigatoni in plate;
spoon in meatballs and sauce to combine. Cover with
wax paper. Microwave at HIGH 5 minutes or until
sauce is bubbly. Sprinkle with additional Parmesan;
cover and let stand 5 minutes before serving.

Makes 4 to 6 servings

Note: Bitty Burgers (meatballs) can be made from almost any burger or meatloaf mixture. Microwave as above or roll into 24 meatballs and pan-fry or broil until meatballs are firm and spring back to the touch.

Pan-fry: In large lightly oiled or nonstick skillet over medium-high heat, brown meatballs 2 minutes. Reduce heat to medium-low and cook 5 to 8 minutes longer, turning occasionally.

Broil: Place meatballs in lightly oiled broiling pan. Broil 5 to 6 inches from heat 8 to 10 minutes, turning occasionally.

Chicken Chow Mein

1 pound boneless skinless chicken
   breasts or thighs
2 cloves garlic, minced
2 tablespoons peanut or vegetable oil,
   divided
¼ cup soy sauce
2 tablespoons dry sherry
6 ounces (2 cups) fresh snow peas or
   1 package (6 ounces) frozen snow
   peas, thawed, cut into halves
3 large green onions, cut diagonally into
   1-inch pieces
6 ounces uncooked Chinese egg noodles
   or vermicelli, cooked, drained and
   rinsed
1 tablespoon Oriental sesame oil

1. Cut chicken crosswise into ¼-inch slices; cut each slice into 1×¼-inch strips. Toss chicken with garlic in small bowl.

2. Heat wok or large skillet over medium-high heat. Add 1 tablespoon peanut oil; heat until hot. Add chicken mixture; stir-fry 3 minutes or until chicken is no longer pink. Transfer to bowl; toss with soy sauce and sherry.

3. Heat remaining 1 tablespoon peanut oil in wok. Add snow peas; stir-fry 2 minutes for fresh or 1 minute for frozen snow peas. Add onions; stir-fry 30 seconds. Add chicken mixture; stir-fry 1 minute.

4. Add noodles to wok; stir-fry 2 minutes or until heated through. Stir in sesame oil; serve immediately.

Makes 4 servings

Turkey and Bow Tie Pasta

¼ cup plus 1 tablespoon flour
2 cups skim milk
1 cup white wine
1 teaspoon Italian seasoning
 Dash pepper
1 pound turkey kielbasa or smoked turkey
  sausage, cut into ½-inch ring slices
1 package (10 ounces) frozen mixed
  vegetables, thawed and drained
6 ounces bow tie pasta, cooked according
  to package directions and drained
 Poppy seeds

1. In medium saucepan combine flour and milk. Add wine, Italian seasoning and pepper, stirring until smooth. Over medium heat cook mixture until thick and bubbly, stirring constantly. Fold in turkey kielbasa, vegetables and pasta; reduce heat to medium-low and cook 5 to 8 minutes or until heated throughout.

2. To serve, top pasta mixture with poppy seeds.

Serves 6

Favorite recipe from **National Turkey Federation**

Microwave Pasta Pie

8 ounces spaghetti, cooked and drained
¼ cup grated Parmesan cheese
1 tablespoon butter or margarine
1 package (1 pound) PERDUE® Fresh
    Sweet or Hot Italian Turkey Sausage
½ cup chopped onion
1 Italian sweet pepper, chopped
1 can (15 ounces) herbed tomato sauce
1 garlic clove, minced
1 tablespoon chopped fresh parsley
½ teaspoon dried basil leaves
½ teaspoon dried oregano leaves
1 package (4 ounces) shredded
    mozzarella cheese

In 10-inch microwave-safe pie plate, place spaghetti.
Add Parmesan cheese and butter; toss until evenly
coated. Arrange pasta on bottom and up sides of plate
to form pasta crust; cover with aluminum foil and set
aside.

In 2½-quart microwave-safe dish, arrange sausage;
cover with wax paper. Microwave at HIGH (100%
power) 4 minutes. Cut sausage into thin slices. Stir in
onion and sweet pepper; cover with wax paper and
microwave at HIGH 3 to 4 minutes, stirring twice.
Drain off pan juices. Stir tomato sauce, garlic, parsley,
basil and oregano into meat mixture; pour into pasta
shell. Sprinkle mozzarella cheese in circle over sauce.
Microwave uncovered at HIGH 1 to 2 minutes until
cheese is melted. Cover with foil and let stand
5 minutes. *Makes 4 to 6 servings*

Manhattan Turkey à la King

8 ounces wide egg noodles
1 pound boneless turkey or chicken, cut
   into strips
1 tablespoon vegetable oil
1 can (14½ ounces) DEL MONTE®
   FreshCut™ Diced Tomatoes with
   Garlic & Onion, undrained
1 can (10¾ ounces) condensed cream of
   celery soup
1 medium onion, chopped
2 stalks celery, sliced
1 cup sliced mushrooms

1. Cook noodles according to package directions;
drain.

2. Brown turkey in oil in large skillet over medium-
high heat. Season with salt and pepper, if desired.

3. Add remaining ingredients except noodles; cover.
Cook 5 minutes. Remove cover; cook 5 minutes or
until thickened, stirring occasionally.

4. Serve over hot noodles. Sprinkle with chopped
parsley, if desired.   *Makes 6 servings*

Helpful Hint: Cook pasta ahead; rinse and drain. Cover
and refrigerate. Just before serving, heat in microwave
or dip in boiling water.

Turkey Tetrazzini

½ pound fresh mushrooms, sliced
¼ cup sliced green onions
1 tablespoon margarine
2 tablespoons flour
¼ teaspoon pepper
1 (12-ounce) can lite evaporated skim milk
⅓ cup low sodium chicken broth
2 tablespoons sherry, optional
8 ounces spaghetti
1 (8-ounce) package HEALTHY CHOICE® Fat Free Natural Shredded Mozzarella Cheese
1 pound (2 cups) turkey breast, cooked, cut into strips

Heat oven to 375°F. Cook mushrooms and green onions in margarine, stirring occasionally, until mushrooms are tender, about 7 minutes. Stir in flour and pepper. Cook and stir 1 minute. Add evaporated milk, chicken broth and sherry. Cook, stirring occasionally, until sauce is thickened. Remove from heat. Cook spaghetti according to package directions. Drain, rinse and keep spaghetti warm. In 2-quart casserole sprayed with non-stick cooking spray layer half of cooked spaghetti, cheese, turkey strips and sauce. Repeat layers with remaining ingredients. Bake at 375°F for 25 to 30 minutes or until bubbly and hot.

Makes 6 servings

Mexican Turkey Chili Mac

1 pound ground turkey

1 package (1¼ ounces) reduced-sodium taco seasoning mix

1 can (14½ ounces) reduced-sodium stewed tomatoes

1 can (11 ounces) corn with red and green peppers, undrained

1½ cups cooked elbow macaroni, without salt, drained

1 ounce low-salt corn chips, crushed

½ cup shredded reduced-fat Cheddar cheese

1. In large nonstick skillet, over medium-high heat, sauté turkey 5 to 6 minutes or until no longer pink; drain. Stir in taco seasoning, tomatoes, corn and macaroni. Reduce heat to medium and cook 4 to 5 minutes until heated throughout.

2. Sprinkle corn chips over meat mixture and top with cheese. Cover and heat 1 to 2 minutes or until cheese is melted. *Makes 6 servings*

Favorite recipe from **National Turkey Federation**

Mexican Turkey Stuffed Shells

  1   **pound ground turkey**
  ½   **cup chopped onions**
  ¼   **cup chopped fresh cilantro**
  1   **teaspoon minced garlic**
  1   **teaspoon dried oregano leaves**
  ½   **teaspoon cumin**
  ½   **teaspoon salt**
  1   **cup non-fat ricotta cheese**
 18   **large pasta shells, uncooked**
  2   **cans (10 ounces each) mild enchilada**
        sauce
  ¼   **cup (1 ounce) shredded reduced-fat**
        Monterey Jack cheese

1. In large bowl, combine turkey, onions, cilantro, garlic, oregano, cumin and salt. Blend in ricotta cheese. Stuff each shell with 1 heaping tablespoonful turkey mixture.

2. In 2-quart oblong glass baking dish, pour 1 can enchilada sauce. Arrange shells in baking dish; dot any remaining turkey mixture over shells. Pour remaining can of sauce over shells; cover tightly with foil. Bake at 375°F 1 to 1¼ hours or until shells are tender. Sprinkle cheese over top. Re-cover and let stand 10 minutes.

Makes 6 servings

Favorite recipe from **National Turkey Federation**

Turkey Shanghai

Nonstick cooking spray
12 ounces turkey breast tenderloin, thinly
sliced
1 cup thinly sliced carrots
½ cup sliced green onions
3 cloves garlic, minced
4 cups ⅓-less-salt chicken broth
6 ounces uncooked angel hair pasta
2 cups frozen French-style green beans
¼ cup plus 2 tablespoons stir-fry sauce
1 teaspoon Oriental sesame oil

1. Spray large nonstick skillet with cooking spray; heat
over medium heat until hot. Add turkey and carrots;
cook and stir 5 minutes or until turkey is no longer
pink. Stir in onions and garlic; cook and stir
2 minutes.

2. Add chicken broth to skillet; bring to a boil over
high heat. Stir in pasta. Return to a boil. Reduce heat
to low. Simmer, uncovered, 5 minutes, stirring
frequently.

3. Stir green beans into skillet. Simmer 2 to 3 minutes
or until pasta is just tender, stirring occasionally.
Remove from heat. Stir in stir-fry sauce and sesame oil.
Let stand 5 minutes. Garnish as desired.

Makes 6 servings

Tortellini with Three-Cheese Tuna Sauce

1   pound cheese-filled tortellini, spinach
      and egg
2   green onions, thinly sliced
1   clove garlic, minced
1   tablespoon butter or margarine
1   cup low-fat ricotta cheese
½   cup low-fat milk
1   can (6 ounces) STARKIST® Tuna,
      drained and broken into chunks
½   cup shredded low-fat mozzarella cheese
¼   cup grated Parmesan or Romano cheese
2   tablespoons chopped fresh basil *or*
      2 teaspoons dried basil, crushed
1   teaspoon grated lemon peel
    Fresh tomato wedges for garnish
      (optional)

Cook tortellini in boiling salted water according to package directions. When tortellini is nearly done, in another saucepan sauté onions and garlic in butter for 2 minutes. Whisk in ricotta cheese and milk. Add tuna, cheeses, basil and lemon peel. Cook over medium-low heat until mixture is heated and cheeses are melted. Drain pasta; add to sauce. Toss well to coat; garnish with tomato wedges if desired. Serve immediately.

Makes 4 to 5 servings

Tuna Vegetable Medley

8 ounces cooked egg noodles
1 package (10 ounces) frozen chopped
  broccoli, thawed and well drained
1 package (10 ounces) frozen carrots,
  thawed and well drained
1 cup corn
1 can (10¾ ounces) cream of mushroom
  soup
1 can (12 ounces) STARKIST® Solid
  White or Chunk Light Tuna, drained
  and chunked
⅔ cup milk
1 cup shredded Swiss, Cheddar or
  Monterey Jack Cheese
  Salt and pepper to taste
¼ cup grated Parmesan cheese

In large bowl, combine all ingredients except Parmesan
cheese; mix well. Pour mixture into 2-quart baking
dish; top with Parmesan cheese. Bake in 400°F oven
20 to 30 minutes or until thoroughly heated and
golden on top.   *Makes 6 servings*

Lemony Dill Salmon and Shell Casserole

  6 ounces uncooked medium shell pasta
    Nonstick cooking spray
1½ cups sliced mushrooms
  ⅓ cup sliced green onions
  1 clove garlic, minced
  2 cups skim milk
  3 tablespoons all-purpose flour
  1 tablespoon grated lemon peel
  ¾ teaspoon dried dill weed
  ¼ teaspoon salt
  ⅛ teaspoon ground black pepper
1½ cups frozen green peas
  1 can (7½ ounces) salmon, drained and
    flaked

1. Preheat oven to 350°F. Cook pasta according to package directions, omitting salt. Rinse; drain. Set aside.

2. Spray medium nonstick saucepan with cooking spray; heat over medium heat until hot. Add mushrooms, onions and garlic; cook and stir 5 minutes or until vegetables are tender.

3. Combine milk and flour in medium bowl until smooth. Stir in lemon peel, dill weed, salt and pepper. Stir into saucepan; heat over medium-high heat 5 to 8 minutes or until thickened, stirring constantly. Remove saucepan from heat. Stir in pasta, peas and salmon. Pour pasta mixture into 2-quart casserole.

4. Bake, covered, 35 to 40 minutes. Serve immediately. Garnish as desired.   *Makes 6 servings*

Linguine with White Clam Sauce

- 8 ounces linguine or spaghetti
- 2 tablespoons butter
- 1 tablespoon flour
- 1 (10-ounce) can clam juice
- 1 tablespoon dried parsley
- 1 teaspoon thyme
- 2 (6.5-ounce) cans minced clams

Prepare pasta according to package directions; drain. Melt the butter in a small saucepan, add flour and mix. Add clam juice and stir until smooth. Add the parsley and thyme; cook over low heat for 5 minutes. Add the clams to the mixture and cook 5 minutes more. Serve over pasta.   *Serves 4*

Favorite recipe from **National Pasta Association**

Skillet Shrimp with Rotelle

3   tablespoons FILIPPO BERIO® Olive
    Oil
1   medium onion, chopped
2   cloves garlic, minced
2   cups uncooked rotelle or other curly
    pasta
3   cups chicken broth
1   cup asparagus tips
¾   pound raw medium shrimp, shelled and
    deveined
¾   cup halved cherry tomatoes
¼   cup pitted ripe olives
1   teaspoon dried oregano leaves
1   teaspoon dried basil leaves
    Salt and freshly ground black pepper

In large skillet, heat olive oil over medium heat until
hot. Add onion and garlic; cook and stir 4 to 6 minutes
or until onion is softened but not brown. Add pasta;
stir to coat pasta with oil. Increase heat to high; pour
in chicken broth. Bring to a boil. Reduce heat to
medium-high; cook, stirring occasionally, 12 to
14 minutes or until pasta is al dente (tender but still
firm). Add asparagus. Cook, stirring frequently, 2 to
3 minutes or until asparagus is tender-crisp. Add
shrimp, tomatoes, olives, oregano and basil. Cook,
stirring frequently, 3 minutes or until liquid is almost
completely absorbed and shrimp are opaque. *Do not
overcook shrimp.* Season to taste with salt and pepper.

Makes 4 to 6 servings

Vegetable Almond Fettuccine

6 tablespoons butter or margarine
2 cloves garlic, minced
2 teaspoons dried basil leaves
1 teaspoon onion powder
¼ teaspoon salt
¼ teaspoon ground black pepper
1 package (9 ounces) fresh spinach
   fettuccine
¾ pound yellow crookneck squash, thinly
   sliced
1 red bell pepper, coarsely chopped
⅔ cup slivered almonds
¼ cup grated Parmesan cheese

1. Melt butter in small nonstick skillet over high heat. Add garlic; reduce heat. Cook 1 minute. Remove from heat; stir in basil, onion powder, salt and black pepper. Keep warm.

2. Bring 3 quarts water to a boil in large saucepan. Add fettuccine, squash and bell pepper. Cook 3 minutes or until vegetables are crisp-tender. Drain; return to saucepan.

3. Pour butter sauce over fettuccine; sprinkle with almonds. Toss well. Transfer to serving bowl.

4. Sprinkle with cheese. Serve immediately.

Makes 4 servings

Cheesy Pasta Swirls

1 bag (16 ounces) frozen vegetable combination (peas, carrots, cauliflower), thawed and drained

1 cup (4 ounces) shredded mozzarella cheese

½ cup (2 ounces) cubed provolone cheese

1⅓ cups (2.8 ounce can) FRENCH'S® French Fried Onions, divided

4 ounces fettuccine, cooked in unsalted water and drained

1 can (10¾ ounces) condensed cream of mushroom soup

¾ cup milk

½ teaspoon garlic salt

⅓ cup (about 1½ ounces) grated Parmesan cheese

Preheat oven to 350°F. In 12×8-inch baking dish, combine vegetables, mozzarella, provolone and ⅔ *cup* French Fried Onions. Twirl a few strands of hot fettuccine around long-tined fork to form a pasta swirl. Remove pasta swirl from fork; stand upright on top of vegetable mixture. Repeat process to form 5 more swirls. In medium bowl, stir together soup, milk and garlic salt; pour over pasta swirls and vegetable mixture. Bake, loosely covered, at 350°F for 30 minutes or until vegetables are done. Top pasta swirls with Parmesan cheese; sprinkle remaining ⅔ *cup* onions around swirls. Bake, uncovered, 5 minutes or until onions are golden brown.   *Makes 6 servings*

Microwave Directions: In 12×8-inch microwave-safe dish, prepare vegetable mixture as above. Form pasta swirls and place on vegetables as above. Prepare soup mixture as above; pour over pasta and vegetables. Cook, loosely covered, on HIGH 14 to 16 minutes or until vegetables are done. Rotate dish halfway through cooking time. Top pasta swirls with Parmesan cheese and remaining onions as above; cook, uncovered, 1 minute. Let stand 5 minutes.

Pasta from the Garden

- 1 **tablespoon olive oil**
- ¾ **cup thinly sliced zucchini**
- 2 **tablespoons chopped green onions**
- 3 **cloves garlic, minced**
- 1 **can (14½ ounces) diced tomatoes, undrained**
- 1 **cup vegetable broth**
- 3 **tablespoons chopped fresh basil** *or* **2 teaspoons dried basil leaves**
- 3 **tablespoons grated Romano cheese**
- 1 **pound penne, cooked and drained**

Heat olive oil in large skillet over medium-high heat until hot. Add zucchini; cook and stir 1 minute. Add onions and garlic; cook and stir 1 minute. Add tomatoes; cook and stir 5 minutes. Add vegetable broth, scraping bottom of skillet clean. Simmer 5 minutes or until broth reduces to ½ cup. Add basil and cheese; stir well. Combine sauce with penne in large bowl; stir gently. *Makes 6 servings*

Cracked Black Pepper Fettuccine with Mushrooms and Zucchini

 1 (12-ounce) package PASTA LABELLA®
    Cracked Black Pepper Fettuccine
 2 tablespoons olive oil
 2 tablespoons butter
 ¾ cup mushrooms, sliced
 ¾ cup zucchini, julienned
 ¼ cup scallions, minced
 ½ tablespoon fresh garlic, sliced
 ¾ cup chicken broth
1½ tablespoons fresh parsley, chopped
    Salt and pepper to taste
 ¼ cup Parmesan cheese, grated

Cook pasta according to package directions.
Meanwhile, heat olive oil and butter in large skillet or
sauté pan. Sauté mushrooms, zucchini and scallions
for 4 minutes. Add garlic, chicken broth and parsley;
simmer for 2 minutes. Season with salt and pepper.
Now add hot fettuccine and toss well with all
ingredients. Sprinkle with Parmesan cheese and serve.

*Serves 4 dinner portions or
6 appetizer portions*

Singapore Spicy Noodles

1¼ cups water
2 tablespoons ketchup
2½ teaspoons packed brown sugar
1½ teaspoons chopped cilantro
1 teaspoon cornstarch
¾ teaspoon LAWRY'S® Seasoned Salt
¾ teaspoon LAWRY'S® Garlic Powder with Parsley
¼ teaspoon crushed red pepper
2½ tablespoons chunky peanut butter
¼ cup sliced green onions
8 ounces linguine, cooked and drained
1 cup shredded red cabbage

In medium saucepan, combine water, ketchup, sugar, cilantro, cornstarch and seasonings. Bring to a boil. Reduce heat; simmer, uncovered, 5 minutes. Cool 10 minutes; blend in peanut butter and green onions. Toss sauce with hot linguine and red cabbage.

Makes 4 servings

Rotini with Summer Vegetables

12 ounces rotini pasta
 3 cups broccoli flowerets
 3 cups sliced carrots
 3 red bell peppers, cut into 1-inch
     squares
 ¼ cup water
 ¼ teaspoon plus ⅛ teaspoon crushed red
     pepper, divided
 3 cups sliced mushrooms
 2 cups (8 ounces) shredded part-skim
     mozzarella cheese
 ¼ cup shredded Asiago cheese
 3 tablespoons olive oil
 3 cloves garlic, minced
 4 cups coarsely chopped, seeded, peeled
     plum tomatoes
 ⅓ cup chopped fresh basil
 ¼ cup Chardonnay or other dry white wine

1. Cook pasta according to package directions; drain. Place in large bowl.

2. Meanwhile, combine broccoli, carrots, bell peppers, water and ¼ teaspoon crushed red pepper in large microwavable baking dish. Cover loosely and microwave at HIGH 5 minutes or until hot. Stir in mushrooms. Cover and microwave 3 minutes. Allow to stand, covered, 5 minutes.

3. Add microwaved vegetables to pasta; toss to combine. Divide mixture between 2 microwavable baking dishes. Sprinkle with cheeses.

4. To prepare sauce, heat olive oil in medium saucepan over medium-low heat until hot. Add garlic and remaining ⅛ teaspoon crushed red pepper. Cook and stir 1 minute. Add tomatoes. Heat 5 minutes. Stir in basil and wine. Simmer 5 minutes.

5. Meanwhile, to heat pasta mixture, microwave each baking dish at MEDIUM-HIGH (80%) 4 to 5 minutes or until heated through. Serve with sauce.

Makes 10 servings

Nokkelost Macaroni & Cheese

- 1 **cup evaporated skim milk**
- 1½ **tablespoons all-purpose flour**
- ½ **cup (2 ounces) shredded NOKKELOST or JARLSBERG Cheese**
- 2 **green onions with tops, sliced**
- 2 **tablespoons chopped pimiento**
- 1 **tablespoon chopped fresh parsley**
- 4 **ounces elbow macaroni, cooked and drained**
- 1 **cup blanched cauliflowerets**
  Salt

In small saucepan over medium heat, gradually add milk to flour, stirring until well blended. Cook until thickened, stirring constantly. Add cheese; stir until melted. Stir in onions, pimiento and parsley. Add to hot macaroni with cauliflowerets; mix lightly. Season with salt to taste.

Makes 4 servings

Pasta Primavera

1 cup carrots, diagonally sliced
1 cup broccoli flowerets
6 ounces fresh pea pods or 1 package
    (6 ounces) frozen pea pods
8 ounces fettuccine
3 cans (14½ ounces each) chicken broth
1 tablespoon dried basil, crushed
1 cup prepared HIDDEN VALLEY
    RANCH® Original Ranch® salad
    dressing
  Romaine lettuce leaves
2 tablespoons grated Parmesan cheese
  Parsley

In large saucepan, steam separately over boiling water carrots, broccoli and pea pods until crisp-tender; cool. In another large saucepan, cook fettuccine in chicken broth until tender; drain and cool. In large bowl, combine vegetables and fettuccine; toss gently. Add basil to salad dressing; mix thoroughly. Add dressing to vegetables and fettuccine; toss to coat. Line salad bowl with lettuce; spoon pasta over lettuce. Top with cheese and parsley.   *Serves 4 to 6*

Classic Macaroni and Cheese

- 2 cups elbow macaroni
- 3 tablespoons butter or margarine
- ¼ cup chopped onion (optional)
- 2 tablespoons all-purpose flour
- ½ teaspoon salt
- ⅛ teaspoon pepper
- 2 cups milk
- 2 cups (8 ounces) SARGENTO® Classic or Fancy Shredded Mild Cheddar Cheese, divided

Cook macaroni according to package directions; drain. In medium saucepan, melt butter and cook onion about 5 minutes or until tender. Stir in flour, salt and pepper. Gradually add milk and cook, stirring occasionally, until thickened. Remove from heat. Add 1½ cups Cheddar cheese and stir until cheese melts. Combine cheese sauce with cooked macaroni. Place in 1½-quart casserole; top with remaining ½ cup Cheddar cheese. Bake at 350°F for 30 minutes or until bubbly and cheese is golden brown.   *Makes 6 servings*

Winter Primavera

1	pound PASTA LABELLA® Angel Hair
⅓	cup extra virgin olive oil
1	cup yellow onions, julienned
¼	cup fresh garlic, sliced thinly
1	cup yellow squash, julienned
1	cup zucchini squash, julienned
1	cup carrots, julienned
1½	cups ripe tomatoes, finely diced
2	teaspoons basil leaves *or* ¼ cup fresh basil, chopped
1	teaspoon oregano leaves
3	cups tomato juice
	Salt and pepper to taste
½	cup Parmesan cheese, grated

Cook pasta according to package directions.
Meanwhile, heat olive oil in a large pot. Sauté onions
and garlic for 3 minutes. Add squash, zucchini and
carrots and cook for 4 minutes. Add diced tomatoes
and herbs and cook for 5 minutes. Add tomato juice
and simmer for 5 additional minutes. Mix hot pasta
with hot primavera sauce. Season with salt and pepper
and sprinkle with Parmesan cheese; serve.

Serves 4 dinner portions or
6 lunch portions

Flash Primavera

1 **pound mostaccioli, ziti or other medium pasta shape, uncooked**
1 **head broccoli or cauliflower, cut into small florets**
1 **tablespoon cornstarch**
¼ **cup water**
3 **cloves garlic, minced**
1 **(15½-ounce) can low-sodium chicken broth**
1 **(10-ounce) package frozen mixed vegetables**
1 **(10-ounce) package frozen chopped spinach, thawed**
  Salt and pepper to taste
1 **cup grated Parmesan cheese**

Prepare pasta according to package directions. Three minutes before pasta is done, stir in broccoli or cauliflower. Drain pasta and vegetables; transfer to large bowl.

In small bowl, dissolve cornstarch in ¼ cup of water. Combine garlic and chicken broth in large saucepan. Simmer over medium heat 3 minutes. Whisk in cornstarch mixture. Stir in mixed vegetables and spinach; cook about 5 minutes or until heated through. Toss sauce and vegetable mixture with pasta. Season with salt and pepper and sprinkle with Parmesan cheese; serve.   *Makes 6 servings*

Favorite recipe from **National Pasta Association**

Saucy Mediterranean Frittata

Tomato Sauce (page 215)
1 tablespoon olive oil
1 small onion, chopped
1 medium tomato, seeded and chopped
1 tablespoon finely chopped fresh basil *or*
    1 teaspoon dried basil leaves, crushed
¼ teaspoon dried oregano leaves, crushed
⅓ cup cooked orzo
⅓ cup chopped pitted ripe olives
8 eggs
½ teaspoon salt
⅛ teaspoon pepper
2 tablespoons butter
½ cup (2 ounces) shredded mozzarella
    cheese

1. Prepare Tomato Sauce.

2. Heat oil in ovenproof 10-inch skillet over medium-high heat. Cook and stir onion in hot oil until tender. Add tomato, basil and oregano; cook and stir 3 minutes. Stir in orzo and olives; remove from skillet and set aside.

3. Beat eggs, salt and pepper in medium bowl with electric mixer at low speed. Stir in tomato mixture; set aside.

4. Melt butter in same skillet over medium heat. Add egg mixture; top with cheese. Reduce heat to low. Cook 8 to 10 minutes or until bottom and most of middle is set.

5. Place skillet on rack 4 inches from broiler. Broil 1 to 2 minutes or until top is browned. Cut into wedges; serve with Tomato Sauce. Garnish as desired. Cut into wedges to serve.   *Makes 4 to 6 servings*

Tomato Sauce

- 1 **can (8 ounces) tomato sauce**
- 1 **teaspoon minced dried onion**
- ¼ **teaspoon dried basil leaves, crushed**
- ¼ **teaspoon dried oregano leaves, crushed**
- ⅛ **teaspoon minced dried garlic**
- ⅛ **teaspoon pepper**

Combine all sauce ingredients in small saucepan. Bring to a boil over high heat. Reduce heat to low. Simmer, uncovered, over medium-low heat 5 minutes, stirring often. Set aside; keep warm.

Makes about 1 cup

Provençal Pasta Shells

12 uncooked jumbo pasta shells
 1 can (6 ounces) pitted ripe olives, drained
 2 tablespoons olive oil
 1 teaspoon lemon juice
 ½ teaspoon dried thyme leaves
1½ cups (6 ounces) shredded Gruyere or mozzarella cheese
 ⅓ cup herb-seasoned bread crumbs
 1 teaspoon bottled minced garlic
 1 jar (14 ounces) commercial chunky spaghetti sauce

1. Cook pasta according to package directions; drain. Rinse with cool water; drain again.

2. While pasta is cooking, combine olives, oil, lemon juice and thyme in food processor; cover and process until puréed. Transfer to small bowl; stir in cheese, bread crumbs and garlic.

3. Spread spaghetti sauce into 11×7×2-inch shallow baking dish. Stuff each pasta shell with 2 tablespoons olive mixture. Arrange stuffed shells on sauce.

4. Cover with plastic wrap, turning back corner to vent. Microwave at HIGH 3 to 4 minutes or until cheese is melted and sauce is hot.

Makes 4 servings

Tomato Basil Pasta Pomadoro Style

1 (12-ounce) package PASTA LABELLA®
  Tomato Basil Pasta
¼ cup extra virgin olive oil
2½ cups tomatoes, diced
¼ cup fresh basil, chopped
2 teaspoons garlic, minced
  Salt and pepper to taste
¾ cup chicken broth
¼ cup Parmesan cheese, grated

Cook pasta according to package directions. Heat olive oil, tomatoes, basil and garlic in large skillet. Season with salt and pepper, and sauté for 4 minutes. Add chicken broth and simmer for 2 minutes. Mix with hot Tomato Basil Pasta, sprinkle with cheese and serve.

Makes 3 dinner or 6 appetizer portions

Straw and Hay Fettuccine

6 ounces plain fettuccine, uncooked
6 ounces spinach fettuccine, uncooked
8 ounces fresh mushrooms, sliced
2 teaspoons margarine
2 cups fresh or frozen peas
4 tablespoons low-fat ricotta cheese
4 tablespoons skim milk
2 tablespoons grated Parmesan cheese

Cook pasta according to package directions; drain and transfer to serving bowl. Sauté mushrooms in margarine in large skillet over low heat 5 minutes. Add peas. Cover; cook until tender. Remove from heat; set aside. In small bowl, combine ricotta cheese, milk and Parmesan cheese. Add cheese mixture to mushrooms and peas. Toss with pasta and serve.

Makes 8 servings

Favorite recipe from **National Pasta Association**

Primavera Tortellini en Brodo

2　cans (about 14 ounces each) reduced-sodium chicken broth
1　package (9 ounces) refrigerated fresh tortellini (cheese, chicken or sausage)
2　cups frozen mixed vegetables, such as broccoli, green beans, onions and red bell peppers
1　teaspoon dried basil leaves
　　Dash hot pepper sauce or to taste
2　teaspoons cornstarch
¼　cup grated Romano or Parmesan cheese

1. Pour broth into large deep skillet. Cover and bring to a boil over high heat. Add tortellini; reduce heat to medium-high. Cook, uncovered, until pasta is tender, stirring occasionally. (Check package directions for approximate timing.)

2. Transfer tortellini to medium bowl with slotted spoon; keep warm. (Do not turn down heat under skillet.)

3. Add vegetables, basil and hot pepper sauce to broth; bring to a boil. Reduce heat to medium; simmer about 3 minutes or until vegetables are crisp-tender.

4. Blend cornstarch and 1 tablespoon water in small cup until smooth. Stir into broth mixture. Cook about 2 minutes or until liquid thickens slightly, stirring frequently. Return tortellini to skillet; heat through. Ladle into shallow soup bowls; sprinkle with cheese.

Makes 2 servings

Good
 Enough

FOR GUESTS

Angel Hair Stir-Fry

1 whole chicken breast, skinned and
    boned
1 tablespoon KIKKOMAN® Stir-Fry Sauce
4 ounces angel hair pasta (capellini)
⅓ cup KIKKOMAN® Stir-Fry Sauce
3 tablespoons water
2 tablespoons vegetable oil, divided
¼ pound fresh snow peas, cut into
    julienne strips
1 large carrot, cut into julienne strips
⅛ teaspoon salt
2 teaspoons sesame seed, toasted

Cut chicken into thin strips; coat with 1 tablespoon
stir-fry sauce. Let stand 30 minutes. Meanwhile, cook
pasta according to package directions, omitting salt.
Drain; rinse under cold water and drain thoroughly.
Combine ⅓ cup stir-fry sauce and water; set aside. Heat
1 tablespoon oil in hot wok or large skillet over high
heat. Add chicken and stir-fry 2 minutes; remove. Heat
remaining 1 tablespoon oil in same pan; add peas and
carrot. Sprinkle vegetables with salt; stir-fry 4 minutes.
Add stir-fry sauce mixture, chicken, pasta and sesame
seed. Cook and stir until all ingredients are coated with
sauce and pasta is heated through.

Makes 4 servings

Mini Meatballs with Pasta and Apple Pesto

PESTO
- 2   cups fresh basil leaves
- 1   Granny Smith apple, peeled, cored and cut into large chunks
- ½   cup grated Parmesan cheese
- ½   cup walnuts
- 1   clove garlic
- 1   teaspoon TABASCO® pepper sauce
- ¼   teaspoon salt
- ¼   cup olive oil
- 8   ounces bow tie pasta

MEATBALLS
- ½   pound lean ground beef
- ½   pound ground turkey
- 1   large egg
- ¼   cup dry seasoned bread crumbs
- ¼   cup club soda
- 1   tablespoon TABASCO® pepper sauce
- ½   cup water
- ½   cup roasted red peppers, cut into strips

• In a food processor or blender, combine basil, apple, cheese, walnuts, garlic, TABASCO® sauce and salt. Gradually add oil until mixture is smooth.

• Prepare bow tie pasta as label directs. Drain.

• Meanwhile, in a large bowl, combine ground beef, turkey, egg, bread crumbs, club soda and TABASCO® sauce until well mixed. Shape mixture into balls, using 1 tablespoon mixture per meatball.

• In a 12-inch nonstick skillet over medium-high heat, cook meatballs until well browned on all sides, turning frequently. Add water to skillet; over high heat, bring to a boil. Reduce heat to low; cover and simmer 10 minutes.

• In a large bowl, toss cooked pasta, pesto sauce, meatballs with their liquid and roasted red pepper strips until well mixed. Serve immediately.

Serves 6

Savory Sausage & Spinach Penne

          8 ounces penne pasta
          2 tablespoons olive oil
          3 cloves garlic, minced
         16 ounces sweet sausage meat, removed
             from casing
         16 ounces fresh leaf spinach
          1 cup crushed tomatoes
         ½ cup chicken broth
         ½ cup white dry wine
         ¾ cup oil packed sundried tomatoes,
             chopped *or* ¼ cup dried sundried
             tomatoes, chopped
          1 tablespoon fresh chopped basil *or*
             1 teaspoon dried basil
          2 teaspoons TABASCO® pepper sauce
             Salt and pepper to taste
             Parmesan cheese to taste

In a medium saucepan, cook pasta and set aside. In a
large skillet over medium-high heat, add oil and garlic;
sauté until garlic is lightly browned. Add crumbled
sausage meat; sauté for 4 minutes then push to the
sides of the pan. Add spinach and sauté until tender,
about 3 minutes. Add crushed tomatoes, chicken
broth, white wine, sundried tomatoes, basil and
TABASCO® sauce; cook for 5 minutes. Remove from
heat; add cooked pasta and toss lightly. Add salt and
pepper to taste. Sprinkle with Parmesan cheese and
serve warm.   *Makes 6 to 8 servings*

Creamy Orzo with Prosciutto

2 tablespoons butter or margarine
2 cloves garlic, minced
1 package (8 ounces) PHILADELPHIA
BRAND® Cream Cheese, cubed
½ cup chicken broth
Dash turmeric
1 package (1 pound) orzo, cooked and
drained
1 package (10 ounces) frozen peas,
thawed and drained
3 ounces thinly sliced prosciutto, cut into
julienne strips
Salt and pepper

• Melt butter in large saucepan over low heat. Add garlic; cook and stir until tender. Add cream cheese, broth and turmeric; stir until cream cheese is melted.

• Stir in orzo, peas and prosciutto; heat thoroughly, stirring occasionally. Season with salt and pepper to taste. Serve with grated Parmesan cheese, if desired.

Makes 8 to 10 servings

Sunday Super Stuffed Shells

1 package (10 ounces) frozen chopped spinach
2 tablespoons olive oil
3 cloves fresh garlic, peeled
¾ pound ground veal
¾ pound ground pork
1 cup parsley, finely chopped
1 cup fresh bread crumbs
2 eggs, beaten
3 cloves fresh garlic, minced
3 tablespoons grated Parmesan cheese
  Salt to taste
1 package (12 ounces) jumbo pasta shells, cooked, drained
3 cups spaghetti sauce

1. Cook spinach according to package directions. Place in colander to drain. Let stand until cool enough to handle. Squeeze spinach between hands to remove excess moisture. Set aside.

2. Heat oil in large skillet over medium heat. Cook and stir whole garlic cloves in hot oil until garlic is lightly browned. Discard garlic. Add veal and pork. Cook until lightly browned, stirring to separate meat; drain drippings. Cool slightly.

3. Preheat oven to 375°F. Grease 12×8-inch baking pan.

4. Combine spinach, parsley, bread crumbs, eggs, minced garlic and cheese in large bowl; blend well. Season to taste with salt. Add cooled meat mixture;

blend well. Fill shells with meat mixture using spoon.

5. Spread about 1 cup spaghetti sauce onto bottom of prepared pan. Arrange shells in pan. Pour remaining sauce over shells. Cover with foil.

6. Bake 35 to 45 minutes or until bubbly. Garnish as desired.   *Makes 8 to 9 servings*

Pasta, Chicken & Broccoli Pesto Toss

4 ounces (about 2 cups) uncooked
   vegetable spiral pasta
2 cups cubed cooked chicken or turkey
   breast meat
2 cups small broccoli florets, cooked
   crisp-tender, cooled
1½ cups (6 ounces) SARGENTO® Light
   Fancy Shredded Mozzarella Cheese
⅔ cup lightly packed fresh basil leaves
2 cloves garlic
1 cup mayonnaise
1 tablespoon lemon juice
½ teaspoon salt
½ cup (1½ ounces) SARGENTO® Fancy
   Shredded Parmesan Cheese
½ cup pine nuts or coarsely chopped
   walnuts, toasted

Cook pasta according to package directions until
tender; drain and cool. Combine pasta, chicken,
broccoli and mozzarella cheese in large bowl. Process
basil and garlic in covered blender or food processor
until finely chopped. Add mayonnaise, lemon juice and
salt. Process to combine thoroughly. Stir in Parmesan
cheese. Add to pasta mixture; toss to coat well. Stir in
pine nuts. Serve immediately or cover and refrigerate.
For maximum flavor, remove from refrigerator and
toss gently 30 minutes before serving.

Makes 8 servings

Sweet Garlic with Chicken Pasta

1 package (16 ounces) bow tie pasta
5½ tablespoons olive oil
8 ounces garlic, finely chopped
1½ pounds shiitake mushrooms, sliced
4 ounces fresh plum tomatoes, seeded
     and chopped
1 cup green onions, chopped
1 teaspoon red pepper flakes
2 cups chicken broth
1¼ pounds boneless skinless chicken
     breast halves, cooked and cut into
     1-inch cubes
4 ounces cilantro, chopped, divided

Cook pasta according to package directions; drain.

Heat oil in large skillet over medium-high heat. Cook
and stir garlic in hot oil until golden. Add mushrooms,
tomatoes, green onions and red pepper flakes. Cook
and stir 2 minutes.

Add broth; simmer mixture to reduce slightly. Add
chicken, pasta and half of cilantro; heat through.
Garnish with remaining cilantro.

Makes 6 to 8 servings

Tomato Basil Pasta

½ cup vegetable oil, divided
¼ cup olive oil
1 teaspoon mustard powder
3 tablespoons balsamic vinegar
2 tablespoons red wine vinegar
2 teaspoons LAWRY'S® Garlic Powder
    with Parsley
2 teaspoons LAWRY'S® Lemon Pepper
1½ teaspoons LAWRY'S® Seasoned Salt
¼ cup marinated sun-dried tomatoes,
    drained and chopped
2 tablespoons chopped fresh basil
4 boneless skinless chicken breast halves
    (¾ to 1 pound), cut into thin strips
1 medium zucchini, cut into julienne
    strips
1 can (2¼ ounces) pitted ripe olives,
    drained
8 ounces penne pasta, cooked, drained
    and kept hot
    Chopped fresh parsley (optional)

In medium bowl, blend ⅓ cup vegetable oil, olive oil,
mustard powder and vinegars with wire whisk. Stir in
Garlic Powder with Parsley, Lemon Pepper, Seasoned
Salt, sun-dried tomatoes and basil. Refrigerate. In
large, deep skillet, heat remaining vegetable oil. Add
chicken; sauté 7 to 10 minutes or until no longer pink
in center, stirring occasionally. Remove chicken from
skillet; set aside. Add zucchini and olives to skillet;
sauté 5 minutes or until zucchini is crisp-tender.

Return chicken to skillet along with hot pasta and enough prepared dressing to coat; toss lightly. Serve with any remaining dressing.

Makes 4 to 6 servings

Presentation: Sprinkle with chopped fresh parsley, if desired.

Hint: Processing dressing in food processor or blender for 1 minute will make a smoother dressing.

Chicken with Pasta and Puttanesca Sauce

8 ounces uncooked ziti or other medium-size pasta

1 package (1½ to 1¾ pounds) GALIL® Chicken Breast Cutlets, split

¼ teaspoon freshly ground black pepper

2 tablespoons olive oil

3 cloves garlic, minced

1 can (14½ ounces) diced tomatoes in juice, undrained

2 tablespoons tomato paste

1 tablespoon drained capers (optional)

1½ teaspoons dried basil leaves

¼ teaspoon crushed red pepper

10 calamata olives, pitted

3 tablespoons chopped fresh Italian parsley (optional)

Cook pasta according to package directions. Do not drain. Set aside. Sprinkle chicken with black pepper. Heat oil in large, deep nonstick skillet over medium-high heat. Add garlic and chicken.

Cook chicken 2 minutes each side or until browned. Reduce heat to medium; add tomatoes with juice, tomato paste, capers, basil and crushed pepper. Simmer, uncovered, 12 to 15 minutes or until chicken is no longer pink in center. Coarsely chop olives; stir into sauce.

Transfer chicken to serving platter. Drain pasta; add to skillet. Toss well. Serve pasta with chicken. Garnish with fresh parsley, if desired. *Makes 4 servings*

Mediterranean Pasta

- 6 to 8 ounces vermicelli
- 2 half boneless chicken breasts, skinned and cut into 1½×½-inch strips
- 4 slices bacon, diced
- 1 can (14½ ounces) DEL MONTE® *FreshCut*™ Diced Tomatoes with Garlic & Onion
- 1 can (15 ounces) DEL MONTE® Tomato Sauce
- ½ teaspoon dried rosemary, crushed
- 1 package (9 ounces) frozen artichoke hearts, thawed
- ½ cup pitted ripe olives, sliced lengthwise

1. Cook pasta according to package directions; drain.

2. Season chicken with salt and pepper, if desired. In large skillet, cook bacon over medium-high heat until almost crisp. Add chicken; cook until browned on both sides. Drain.

3. Stir in tomatoes, tomato sauce and rosemary. Cook 15 minutes, stirring occasionally. Add artichokes and olives; heat through.

4. Spoon sauce over hot pasta just before serving. Sprinkle with crumbled feta cheese and chopped parsley, if desired.   *4 to 6 servings*

Helpful Hint: Cook pasta ahead; rinse and drain. Cover and refrigerate. Just before serving, heat in microwave or dip into boiling water.

California Walnut Noodles

DRESSING

 ½ cup plain nonfat yogurt
 ½ cup orange juice
 3 tablespoons balsamic vinegar or wine
   vinegar
 2 tablespoons brown sugar
 2 teaspoons sesame oil
 1½ teaspoons grated fresh ginger *or*
   ½ teaspoon ground ginger
 ½ teaspoon crushed red pepper (optional)
 2 cloves garlic, minced
   Salt to taste (optional)

NOODLES

 12 ounces uncooked spaghetti or linguine
 2 cups cooked, diced skinless chicken
   breasts
 1 red or green bell pepper, halved, seeded
   and thinly sliced
 1 cucumber, halved, seeded and thinly
   sliced
 ½ cup chopped green onions
 2 teaspoons minced jalapeño pepper or
   other hot chili pepper
 2 tablespoons chopped cilantro (optional)
 ⅔ cup Savory California Walnut Sprinkles
   (page 235)

For dressing, whisk together yogurt, orange juice,
vinegar, sugar, oil, ginger, crushed red pepper, garlic
and salt in large bowl. Set aside.

Cook pasta according to package directions. Drain and rinse well; drain again. Toss pasta and ¾ cup dressing in large bowl. Combine chicken, bell pepper, cucumber, green onions, jalapeño pepper and cilantro with remaining dressing. Arrange pasta on large platter or in shallow bowl. Spoon chicken mixture in center. Just before serving, top each serving with ¼ of the walnut sprinkles.

Makes 4 servings

Savory California Walnut Sprinkles

- 4 ounces (1 cup) chopped California walnuts
- ½ cup fresh white bread crumbs
- 1 tablespoon paprika
- ¼ teaspoon cayenne pepper
- ¼ teaspoon salt (optional)

Preheat oven to 325°F. In food processor, process walnuts until finely ground; transfer to small bowl. Add bread crumbs; stir to combine. Spread mixture in even layer on ungreased baking sheet. Bake 15 minutes, stirring frequently, until mixture is golden brown and crisp. Stir in paprika, cayenne pepper and salt. Cool to room temperature.

Makes 1¼ cups

Favorite recipe from **Walnut Marketing Board**

Jerk Chicken and Pasta

Jerk Sauce (page 237)
12 ounces boneless skinless chicken breasts
Nonstick cooking spray
1 cup fat-free reduced-sodium chicken broth
1 green bell pepper, sliced
2 green onions, sliced
8 ounces fettuccine, cooked and kept warm
Grated Parmesan cheese (optional)

1. Spread Jerk Sauce on both sides of chicken. Place in glass dish; refrigerate, covered, 15 to 30 minutes.

2. Spray skillet with cooking spray. Heat over medium heat until hot. Add chicken; cook 5 to 10 minutes until no longer pink in center. Add chicken broth, bell pepper and onions; bring to a boil. Reduce heat; simmer, uncovered, 5 to 7 minutes or until vegetables are crisp-tender and broth is reduced to thin sauce consistency. Remove chicken from skillet; cut into slices. Toss pasta, chicken and vegetable mixture in bowl. Sprinkle with Parmesan cheese, if desired.

Makes 4 servings

Jerk Sauce

2 tablespoons lime juice
¼ cup loosely packed fresh cilantro
2 tablespoons coarsely chopped fresh
    ginger
3 cloves garlic
2 tablespoons black pepper
1 tablespoon ground allspice
½ teaspoon curry powder
¼ teaspoon ground cloves
⅛ teaspoon ground red pepper

1. Combine all ingredients in food processor or blender; process until thick paste consistency.

Makes about ¼ cup

Chicken and Tomatoes in Red Pepper Cream

9   ounces refrigerated angel hair pasta
1   jar (7 ounces) roasted red peppers,
      drained
⅓   cup half-and-half
2   teaspoons Dijon mustard
1   teaspoon salt
12 sun-dried tomatoes (packed in oil),
      drained
1   tablespoon olive oil
4   boneless skinless chicken breast halves
      (about 1 pound)
    Grated Parmesan cheese

1. Cook pasta according to package directions; drain.

2. While the pasta is cooking, combine red peppers, half-and-half, mustard and salt in food processor or blender; cover and process until smooth. Set aside.

3. Rinse tomatoes in warm water; drain and pat dry. Cut in half.

4. Heat olive oil in large skillet over medium-high heat until hot. Add chicken and tomatoes. Cook chicken, uncovered, 3 minutes per side.

5. Add red pepper mixture. Simmer 3 minutes or until sauce thickens slightly and chicken is no longer pink in center. Season to taste with freshly ground black pepper.

6. Serve chicken and sauce over pasta. Sprinkle with Parmesan cheese.   *Makes 4 servings*

Rotelle with Grilled Chicken Dijon

¾ cup **GREY POUPON®** Dijon Mustard, divided
1 tablespoon lemon juice
1 tablespoon olive oil
1 clove garlic, minced
½ teaspoon Italian seasoning
1 pound boneless, skinless chicken breasts
¼ cup margarine or butter
1 cup **COLLEGE INN®** Chicken Broth or Lower Sodium Chicken Broth
1 cup chopped cooked broccoli
⅓ cup coarsely chopped roasted red peppers
1 pound tricolor rotelle or spiral-shaped pasta, cooked
¼ cup grated Parmesan cheese

In medium bowl, combine ¼ cup mustard, lemon juice, oil, garlic and Italian seasoning. Add chicken, stirring to coat well. Refrigerate for 1 hour.

Grill or broil chicken over medium heat for 6 minutes on each side or until done. Cool slightly; slice into ½-inch strips and set aside.

In large skillet, over medium heat, melt margarine or butter; blend in remaining mustard and chicken broth. Stir in broccoli and peppers; heat through. In large serving bowl, combine hot cooked pasta, broccoli mixture, chicken and Parmesan cheese, tossing to coat well. Garnish as desired. Serve immediately.

Makes 5 servings

Turkey Manicotti

1 pound Italian turkey sausage
¼ pound fresh mushrooms, chopped
½ cup chopped onion
1 clove garlic, minced
1 cup (4 ounces) shredded part-skim
    mozzarella cheese
1½ cups low-fat ricotta cheese
1 egg, beaten
1 package (10 ounces) frozen chopped
    spinach, thawed and well drained
1 package (8 ounces) manicotti shells,
    cooked according to package
    directions and drained
    Vegetable cooking spray
¼ cup flour
⅛ teaspoon pepper
1 can (15 ounces) evaporated skim milk
½ cup low-sodium chicken broth
½ cup plus 2 tablespoons grated
    Parmesan cheese

1. In large nonstick skillet over medium heat, cook and stir turkey sausage, mushrooms, onion and garlic 5 to 6 minutes or until sausage is no longer pink. Remove skillet from heat and drain.

2. In large bowl, combine mozzarella cheese, ricotta cheese and egg. Add turkey sausage mixture and spinach; mix well.

3. Cut each manicotti shell open down long side. (This will make stuffing shells easier.) Carefully spoon about ⅓ cup turkey sausage filling down center of each shell; roll up shell to enclose filling. Arrange stuffed shells, seam side down, in 14×11-inch baking dish lightly coated with vegetable spray.

4. In medium saucepan, combine flour and pepper. Gradually add evaporated milk and chicken broth, stirring with wire whisk until well blended. Cook over medium heat, stirring constantly, until sauce comes to a boil and thickens. Remove pan from heat; whisk in ½ cup Parmesan cheese. Pour sauce over stuffed shells; sprinkle with remaining Parmesan cheese.

5. Cover baking pan with foil. Bake in 350°F oven 20 to 25 minutes or until mixture is heated through.

Makes 8 servings

Favorite recipe from **National Turkey Federation**

Turkey Shanghai

1 package (about 1¼ pounds) PERDUE®
FIT 'N EASY® Fresh Skinless and
Boneless Turkey Breast Tenderloins
½ cup white wine, divided
3 tablespoons reduced-sodium soy sauce,
divided
1 tablespoon cornstarch
Ground pepper to taste
1 tablespoon sugar
2 teaspoons rice vinegar or white vinegar
1½ tablespoons vegetable oil
1 garlic clove, minced
1 teaspoon minced fresh ginger
2 carrots, shredded
⅓ pound green beans, split lengthwise and
lightly steamed
½ cup thinly sliced scallions
2 cups hot cooked Chinese noodles
(optional)
Carrots and scallions cut in flower
shapes (optional)
Cilantro sprigs (optional)

Slice turkey into thin strips; place in medium bowl.
Sprinkle with ¼ cup wine, 1 tablespoon soy sauce,
cornstarch and pepper; toss to coat. Marinate at room
temperature 15 minutes. In small bowl, combine
remaining ¼ cup wine, 2 tablespoons soy sauce, sugar
and vinegar; set aside.

Over medium-high heat, heat a wok or large, heavy nonstick skillet. Slowly add oil; stir in garlic, ginger and turkey. Stir-fry 3 to 4 minutes until turkey is cooked through. Add carrots, beans, scallions and reserved wine mixture; cook 1 to 2 minutes longer. Serve over Chinese noodles; garnish with carrot and scallion flowers and cilantro sprigs.

Makes 4 servings

Pasta Verde de Mar

1 pound cod fillets
1 (13¾-ounce) can chicken broth
8 ounces packaged spinach linguine or
   fettucini
3 tablespoons olive oil
2 cloves garlic, crushed
6 green onions, bias sliced into ½-inch
   pieces
1 yellow pepper, cut in ¼-inch strips
½ cup fresh basil, chopped *or*
   1 tablespoon dried basil, crushed
¼ teaspoon red pepper flakes
8 cherry tomatoes, cut into quarters
¼ cup parsley, chopped
1 (8-ounce) jar sun-dried tomatoes
   (optional)

Place cod fillets in a 10-inch skillet with chicken broth. (If desired, add 1 slice lemon, 1 bay leaf and a few peppercorns to liquid.) Bring liquid to a boil; cover and immediately reduce heat. Simmer for 8 to 10 minutes or until fish becomes opaque. As fish simmers, cook pasta according to package directions; drain and toss with 1 tablespoon olive oil. Keep pasta warm.

Remove cooked fish from skillet; keep warm. Pour off cooking liquid, reserving ½ cup. Pre-heat dry skillet over high heat; add remaining olive oil. Add garlic, green onions, yellow pepper, basil and pepper flakes; stir-fry 3 to 5 minutes or until vegetables are tender-crisp. Remove pan from heat. Add tomatoes, parsley and sun-dried tomatoes, if desired; mix well.

Use a fork to break cod into 2-inch pieces; add fish and reserved cooking liquid to vegetables. Add pasta to skillet and toss gently with two forks to combine. Serve immediately. *Makes 4 servings*

Favorite recipe from **National Fisheries Institute**

Salmon, Fettuccine & Cabbage

1   (9-ounce) package fresh fettuccine
¼   cup plus 2 tablespoons seasoned rice
      vinegar
2   tablespoons vegetable oil
½   small head of cabbage, shredded (about
      7 cups)
½   teaspoon fennel seeds
1   (15½-ounce) can salmon, drained,
      flaked, bones removed
      Salt and pepper

1. Cook fettuccine in lightly salted boiling water according to package directions (about 5 minutes); drain.

2. Heat vinegar and oil in large skillet over medium-high heat. Add cabbage; cook 3 minutes or until crisp-tender, stirring occasionally.

3. Stir in fennel seeds. Add fettuccine; toss lightly to coat. Add salmon; mix lightly.

4. Heat thoroughly, stirring occasionally. Season with salt and pepper to taste. Garnish as desired.

Makes 4 servings

Basil-Pecan Shells with Smoked Salmon

    1   cup fresh basil, stems removed
    ¼   cup freshly grated Parmesan cheese
    2   cloves garlic
    1   tablespoon olive oil
    ¾   cup plain nonfat yogurt
    ⅓   cup skim milk
   12   ounces uncooked medium-size pasta
        shells or conchiglie
    8   ounces smoked salmon, cut into bite-
        size pieces
    4   tablespoons chopped pecans, toasted

1. Place basil, Parmesan, garlic and oil in food processor or blender; process until finely chopped. Set aside.

2. Combine yogurt and milk in small bowl; set aside.

3. Cook pasta according to package directions, omitting salt. Drain well. Transfer to large serving bowl. Add basil mixture, yogurt mixture, salmon and pecans. Mix well. Garnish as desired. Serve immediately.   *Makes 4 servings*

Golden Apple-Salmon Pasta

8 ounces salmon, thawed if necessary, cut
   into ¾-inch chunks*
2 tablespoons butter or margarine,
   divided
1 cup sliced mushrooms
¾ cup diagonally sliced asparagus**
¼ cup chopped onion
¼ teaspoon oregano, crushed
⅛ teaspoon each salt and pepper
⅓ cup half-and-half
1 Golden Delicious apple, cored and diced
4 ounces fettuccine noodles or spaghetti,
   cooked and drained
   Grated Parmesan cheese

Sauté salmon in 1 tablespoon butter 5 minutes or until
barely cooked; remove from skillet. Sauté mushrooms,
asparagus and onion in remaining 1 tablespoon butter
for 2 minutes. Add seasonings and half-and-half; cook
and stir on high heat 1 minute. Add apple and salmon;
cook and stir 30 seconds or until vegetables are tender
and salmon flakes easily when tested with fork. Serve
over hot fettuccine. Sprinkle with Parmesan cheese.

Makes 2 or 3 servings

*Eight ounces tiny pink shrimp can be substituted for salmon.

**One-half cup thawed frozen peas can be substituted for asparagus.
Add peas with apple.

Note: Recipe may be doubled.

Favorite recipe from **Washington Apple Commission**

Albacore and Asparagus Pasta

½   **pound uncooked angel hair pasta**
1   **tablespoon olive oil**
1   **can (10¾ ounces) cream of asparagus
     soup**
¾   **cup half & half**
1   **can (6 ounces) STARKIST® Solid
     White Tuna, drained and chunked**
½   **pound asparagus, trimmed, cut into
     1-inch pieces and blanched *or*
     1 package (10 ounces) frozen
     asparagus, thawed and drained**
½   **teaspoon lemon juice
     Freshly ground black pepper to taste**
¼   **cup grated Parmesan cheese**
1   **tablespoon minced fresh parsley**

Cook pasta according to package directions; drain and
toss with olive oil. Keep warm. Meanwhile, in medium
saucepan, combine soup and half & half; blend well.
Stir in tuna, blanched asparagus, lemon juice and
black pepper. Heat thoroughly; serve over pasta.
Sprinkle with cheese and parsley.

Makes 2 servings

Spicy Tuna and Linguine with Garlic and Pine Nuts

- 2 tablespoons olive oil
- 4 cloves garlic, minced
- 2 cups sliced mushrooms
- ½ cup chopped onion
- ½ teaspoon crushed red pepper
- 2½ cups chopped plum tomatoes
- 1 can (14½ ounces) chicken broth plus water to equal 2 cups
- ½ teaspoon salt
- ¼ teaspoon coarsely ground black pepper
- 1 package (9 ounces) uncooked fresh linguine
- 1 can (12 ounces) STARKIST® Solid White Tuna, drained and chunked
- ⅓ cup chopped fresh cilantro
- ⅓ cup toasted pine nuts or almonds

In 12-inch skillet, heat olive oil over medium-high heat; sauté garlic, mushrooms, onion and red pepper until golden brown. Add tomatoes, chicken broth mixture, salt and black pepper; bring to a boil.

Separate uncooked linguine into strands; place in skillet and spoon sauce over. Reduce heat to simmer; cook, covered, 4 more minutes or until cooked through. Toss gently; add tuna and cilantro and toss again. Sprinkle with pine nuts.

Makes 4 to 6 servings

Crab Basil Fettuccine

3 tablespoons margarine or butter
3 tablespoons olive oil
2 tomatoes, peeled, seeded, chopped
1 garlic clove, minced
⅓ cup whipping cream
½ cup HOLLAND HOUSE® White Cooking
  Wine
½ cup chopped fresh basil
½ cup cooked fresh or frozen crabmeat
¼ cup freshly grated Parmesan cheese
¼ cup chopped fresh parsley
1 pound fettuccine, cooked, drained

Melt margarine and oil in medium saucepan over
medium heat. Add tomatoes and garlic; simmer until
tomatoes are softened. Add whipping cream and
cooking wine; simmer 10 minutes. Stir in basil and
crabmeat; simmer 3 minutes. Add ½ of cheese and ½ of
parsley. Serve over cooked fettuccine. Sprinkle with
remaining cheese and parsley.   *6 servings*

Scallops with Linguine and Spinach

- 2 to 3 tablespoons olive oil
- 1½ cups finely chopped onion
- 2 tablespoons minced garlic
- ⅛ to ¼ teaspoon cayenne pepper
- 1 cup slivered red bell pepper
- ⅓ cup fresh lemon juice
- 1 tablespoon brown sugar
- 1 tablespoon minced lemon zest
- 1 teaspoon salt
- 1 teaspoon black pepper
- ¾ pound cooked linguine
- 1 (10-ounce) package frozen chopped spinach, thawed and drained
- 1½ pounds cooked scallops
- ⅓ cup feta cheese, coarsely chopped

Heat oil in 12-inch heavy skillet on medium-low heat until hot. Add onion, garlic, cayenne and bell pepper; cook, uncovered, until tender, about 10 minutes. Add lemon juice, brown sugar, zest, salt and pepper; heat 1 minute.

While preparing onion mixture, bring a large pot of water to a boil; salt to taste. Cook pasta until tender, 8 to 10 minutes. About 1 minute before pasta is cooked, add spinach. Drain pasta and spinach; place in a large warm serving bowl. Add onion mixture and toss to coat. Taste and adjust seasonings. Add cooked and warmed scallops to pasta and sprinkle with feta cheese.

Makes 4 servings

Favorite recipe from **National Fisheries Institute**

Winter Pesto Pasta with Shrimp

12 ounces fettuccine, uncooked
1 cup chopped fresh kale, washed, stems removed
½ cup fresh basil
¼ cup grated Parmesan cheese
2 cloves garlic, halved
⅛ teaspoon salt
1 cup plain nonfat yogurt
1 teaspoon vegetable oil
1 pound medium shrimp, peeled, deveined
1 medium red bell pepper, cut into bite-size pieces

Cook pasta according to package directions. While pasta is cooking, purée kale, basil, Parmesan cheese, garlic and salt in food processor or blender until smooth. Stir in yogurt.

Heat oil in large skillet over medium-low heat. Sauté shrimp and bell pepper 4 minutes or until shrimp are opaque.

When pasta is done, drain and transfer to serving bowl. Add kale mixture; toss well. Add shrimp and bell pepper; toss gently. Serve immediately.

Makes 4 servings

Favorite recipe from **National Pasta Association**

Creamy Seafood Pasta

 1   tablespoon margarine or butter
 2   tablespoons all-purpose flour
2¼ cups hot milk
 ⅔   cup GREY POUPON® COUNTRY
       DIJON® Mustard
 2   tablespoons chopped parsley
 1   tablespoon chopped fresh dill weed
 1   tablespoon lemon juice
 1   pound medium shrimp, cleaned and
       cooked
 1   cup frozen peas
 1   pound bow tie pasta (farfalle), cooked
 1   cup cherry tomatoes, halved
 ⅓   cup grated Parmesan cheese

In large saucepan, over medium heat, melt margarine
or butter. Blend in flour; cook 2 to 3 minutes.
Gradually whisk in milk; cook and stir until mixture
thickens and boils. Reduce heat; simmer for 3 to 4
minutes. Whisk in mustard, parsley, dill and lemon
juice; cook 1 minute. Stir in shrimp and peas; heat
through.

In large serving bowl, combine hot cooked pasta,
shrimp mixture, tomatoes and Parmesan cheese,
tossing to coat well. Serve immediately.

Makes 5 servings

Pasta with Hearts

- 8 ounces mostaccioli, rotini, or other medium pasta shape, uncooked
- 1 (8-ounce) jar roasted red peppers, drained
- ¼ teaspoon hot red pepper flakes
- 4 to 6 drops red pepper sauce
- 2 cloves garlic
- 2 teaspoons balsamic vinegar
- 4 teaspoons vegetable or olive oil
- ¼ cup white wine
- ½ cup non-fat plain yogurt
- 8 ounces shrimp, shelled and steamed or boiled
- 1 (8½-ounce) can artichoke hearts, drained

Cook pasta according to package directions; drain. In a food processor or blender, combine the jar of red peppers with the hot red pepper flakes, red pepper sauce, garlic and vinegar. Purée until smooth.

Transfer the mixture to a small sauté pan; heat through. Add oil; stir to combine. Add the white wine and simmer until the mixture reduces. Just before serving, stir in the yogurt until warmed through. Remove from heat. In a large mixing bowl, toss together the cooked pasta, shrimp, artichoke hearts and yogurt dressing. Serve immediately.

Serves 4

Favorite recipe from **National Pasta Association**

Tasty Thai Shrimp & Sesame Noodles

- 1 **pound medium shrimp, shelled and deveined**
- 1 **(8-ounce) bottle NEWMAN'S OWN® Light Italian Dressing**
- 2 **tablespoons chunky peanut butter**
- 1 **tablespoon soy sauce**
- 1 **tablespoon honey**
- 1 **teaspoon grated peeled gingerroot**
- ½ **teaspoon crushed red pepper**
- 1 **(8-ounce) package capellini or angel hair pasta**
- 2 **tablespoons salad oil**
- 1 **tablespoon sesame oil**
- 1 **medium carrot, peeled and shredded**
- 1 **cup chopped green onions**
- ¼ **cup chopped fresh cilantro for garnish**

In medium bowl, mix shrimp with ⅓ cup Newman's Own® Light Italian Dressing. Cover and refrigerate 1 hour. In small bowl, with wire whisk or fork, mix peanut butter, soy sauce, honey, ginger, crushed red pepper and remaining dressing; set aside. After shrimp has marinated 1 hour, prepare capellini as label directs; drain.

Meanwhile, in 4-quart saucepan over high heat, heat salad oil and sesame oil until very hot. In hot oil, cook carrot 1 minute. Drain off dressing from shrimp; discard dressing. Add shrimp and green onions to carrot; cook, stirring constantly, approximately 3 minutes or until shrimp turn opaque throughout. In large bowl, toss hot capellini with dressing mixture and shrimp mixture. Sprinkle with chopped cilantro.

Serves 4

Hombre Shrimp and Fettucini with Salsa Pesto

      1 cup NEWMAN'S OWN® Salsa (medium
         or hot)
      2 tablespoons fresh lemon juice
      2 cloves garlic, minced
      ½ teaspoon salt
     20 large shrimp, peeled, deveined and tails
         left intact
      1 pound fettucini, cooked al dente and
         drained
         Parmesan cheese
         Lemon wedges and parsley sprigs

SALSA PESTO
      ¾ cup NEWMAN'S OWN® Salsa (medium
         or hot)
      2 cloves garlic, minced
   1¼   cups firmly packed, rinsed, stemmed
         and drained, spinach leaves
      ½ cup fresh cilantro*
      ½ cup grated Parmesan cheese
      ¾ cup toasted pine nuts
      ⅓ cup olive oil

Combine 1 cup Newman's Own® Salsa, lemon juice,
minced garlic and salt in glass mixing bowl.
Rinse shrimp and pat dry. Thread onto 4 soaked
wooden skewers; grill or broil 5 to 8 minutes or until
shrimp is cooked through, turning and basting
occasionally with sauce. Keep shrimp and remaining
sauce warm.

For pesto, place ¼ cup salsa, garlic, spinach, cilantro, ½ cup Parmesan cheese, ½ cup pine nuts and oil in blender. Cover; purée until thick and smooth. Transfer pesto into large mixing bowl; stir in remaining salsa. Add warm fettucini; toss to coat.

Evenly divide fettucini mixture between 4 individual serving plates. Sprinkle reserved pine nuts over each portion. Top each with a warm shrimp skewer. Serve with warm sauce. Sprinkle with Parmesan cheese; garnish with lemon wedges and parsley sprigs.

Serves 4

*Basil can be substituted for the cilantro, if preferred.

Shrimp Creole Pronto

2   tablespoons oil
1   cup chopped onions
1   cup chopped celery
1   green bell pepper, chopped
2   garlic cloves, minced
2   cups chopped peeled tomatoes
1   (8-ounce) can tomato sauce
½   cup HOLLAND HOUSE® Marsala
      Cooking Wine
¼   to ½ teaspoon hot pepper sauce
¼   teaspoon freshly ground black pepper
1   pound fresh or frozen uncooked
      shrimp, peeled, deveined
1   (10-ounce) package egg noodles,
      cooked, drained or hot cooked rice

Heat oil in large saucepan over medium-high heat. Add
onions, celery, green pepper and garlic; cook 2 to 3
minutes. Add tomatoes; cook 2 to 3 minutes, stirring
occasionally. Add remaining ingredients except
noodles; cook 2 to 3 minutes or until shrimp turn
pink. Serve over cooked noodles or hot cooked rice.

4 servings

Stuffed Shells

8 jumbo pasta shells (1 pound)
6 ounces (1 carton) ALPINE LACE® Fat
    Free Cream Cheese with Garlic &
    Herbs
¼ cup fat free sour cream
½ cup Italian seasoned dry bread crumbs
2 tablespoons slivered fresh basil leaves
1 small ripe tomato, finely chopped
1 cup marinara sauce (bottled or
    refrigerated), heated (optional)

1. Cook the pasta shells according to package directions until al dente. Drain well; arrange on a serving platter and keep warm.

2. Meanwhile, in a small saucepan, stir the cream cheese and the sour cream over low heat until hot. (Do not boil.) Remove from the heat and stir in the bread crumbs and basil.

3. Using a small spoon, stuff each shell with the cheese mixture, then top with a few pieces of tomato. Serve immediately with the marinara sauce, if desired.

Makes 4 servings (2 stuffed shells each)

Pasta with Onions and Goat Cheese

-----

2 teaspoons olive oil
4 cups thinly sliced sweet onions
¾ cup (3 ounces) goat cheese
¼ cup skim milk
6 ounces uncooked baby bow tie or other
   small pasta
1 clove garlic, minced
2 tablespoons dry white wine or fat-free
   reduced-sodium chicken broth
1½ teaspoons chopped fresh sage *or*
   ½ teaspoon dried sage leaves
½ teaspoon salt
¼ teaspoon pepper
2 tablespoons chopped toasted walnuts

Heat oil in large nonstick skillet over medium heat. Add onions; cook slowly until golden and carmelized, about 20 to 25 minutes, stirring occasionally.

Combine goat cheese and milk in small bowl; stir until well blended. Set aside.

Cook pasta according to package directions, omitting salt. Drain and set aside.

Add garlic to onions in skillet; cook until softened, about 3 minutes. Add wine, sage, salt and pepper; cook until moisture is evaporated. Remove from heat; add pasta and goat cheese mixture, stirring to melt cheese. Sprinkle with walnuts. *Makes 8 (½-cup) servings*

Hearty Manicotti

8 to 10 dried manicotti shells, cooked, drained
1¾ cups (15-ounce container) ricotta cheese
1 package (10 ounces) frozen chopped spinach, thawed, squeezed dry
½ cup (2 ounces) grated Parmesan cheese
1 egg
⅛ teaspoon ground black pepper
1⅓ cups (*two* 6-ounce cans) CONTADINA® Dalla Casa Buitoni Italian Paste with Roasted Garlic
1⅓ cups water
½ cup (2 ounces) shredded mozzarella cheese

COMBINE ricotta cheese, spinach, Parmesan cheese, egg and pepper in medium bowl. Spoon mixture into manicotti shells. Place in 12×7-inch baking dish.

STIR together tomato paste and water in medium bowl; pour over manicotti. Sprinkle with mozzarella cheese.

BAKE, uncovered, in preheated 350°F. oven for 30 to 40 minutes or until heated through.

Makes 4 to 5 servings

Fettuccine with Olive Pesto

- 10 ounces dried fettuccine
- 1½ cups whole pitted California ripe olives
- 3 tablespoons drained capers
- 4 teaspoons lemon juice
- 1 tablespoon olive oil
- 2 teaspoons Dijon mustard
- 2 to 3 cloves garlic, peeled
- ¼ cup finely chopped fresh basil
- ¼ cup grated Parmesan cheese
  Basil sprigs

Cook fettuccine according to package directions. While pasta cooks, combine olives, capers, lemon juice, oil, mustard and garlic in a food processor or blender. Whirl until coarsely puréed. Stir in chopped basil and cheese; set aside. Drain pasta well and transfer to a large warm serving bowl. Spoon pesto over pasta and mix gently. Garnish with basil sprigs.

Makes 4 servings

Favorite recipe from **California Olive Industry**

Fettuccine with Sun-Dried Tomato Cream

⅔ cup sun-dried tomatoes
3 to 4 garlic cloves
1 (8-ounce) container PHILADELPHIA
    BRAND® Soft Cream Cheese
½ teaspoon dried oregano leaves, crushed
¼ cup butter or margarine
¼ cup BREAKSTONE'S® sour cream
1 pound fettuccine, cooked, drained, kept
    warm
¼ cup olive oil
    Salt and pepper
2 tablespoons chopped fresh parsley

• Cover tomatoes with boiling water; let stand 10 minutes. Drain.

• Place tomatoes and garlic in food processor or blender container; process until coarsely chopped. Add cream cheese and oregano; process until well blended.

• Melt butter in medium saucepan; stir in cream cheese mixture and sour cream. Cook until thoroughly heated.

• Toss warm fettuccine with oil.

• Add cream cheese mixture. Season to taste with salt and pepper. Sprinkle with chopped parsley. Serve immediately.   *Makes 8 to 10 servings*

Fettuccine Gorgonzola with Sun-Dried Tomatoes

8   ounces uncooked spinach or tricolor
    fettuccine
1   cup low fat cottage cheese
½   cup plain nonfat yogurt
½   cup (2 ounces) crumbled Gorgonzola
    cheese
⅛   teaspoon ground white pepper
2   cups rehydrated sun-dried tomatoes
    (4 ounces dry), cut into strips

1. Cook pasta according to package directions, omitting salt. Drain well. Cover to keep warm.

2. Combine cottage cheese and yogurt in food processor or blender; process until smooth. Heat cottage cheese mixture in small saucepan over low heat. Add Gorgonzola and white pepper; stir until cheese is melted.

3. Return pasta to saucepan; add tomatoes. Pour cheese mixture over pasta; mix well. Garnish as desired. Serve immediately.   *Makes 4 servings*

Penne with Creamy Tomato Sauce

8 ounces dried penne pasta, cooked, drained and kept warm
1 tablespoon olive oil
½ cup chopped onion
2 tablespoons dry vermouth or white wine
1¾ cups (14.5-ounce can) CONTADINA® Dalla Casa Buitoni Pasta Ready Chunky Tomatoes with Olive Oil, Garlic & Spices, undrained
1 cup (3.8-ounce can) sliced ripe olives, drained
½ cup heavy whipping cream
½ cup (2 ounces) grated Parmesan cheese
Sliced green onions

HEAT oil in large skillet over medium-high heat. Add onion; cook for 2 minutes. Add vermouth; cook for 1 minute. Add pasta, tomatoes and juice, olives, cream and cheese; toss well. Cook for 2 to 3 minutes. Sprinkle with green onions.   *Makes 4 servings*

Porcini Mushroom Penne Rigate with Garlic Butter Sauce

1   (12-ounce) package of PASTA LABELLA®
    Porcini Mushroom Penne Rigate
1   tablespoon extra virgin olive oil
2   tablespoons butter
2   teaspoons garlic, minced
1½ cups mushrooms, chopped
¾   cup white wine
2   tablespoons lemon juice
¼   cup scallions, minced
1½ tablespoons parsley, chopped
¼   cup Parmesan cheese, grated

Cook pasta according to package directions. Heat olive oil and butter in large skillet; sauté garlic and mushrooms over medium heat for 4 minutes. Add wine, lemon juice and scallions to skillet; simmer. Mix in hot Porcini Mushroom Penne Rigate; sprinkle with parsley and cheese before serving.

Makes 3 dinner or 6 appetizer portions

Tangy Asparagus Linguine

5 ounces linguine
2 tablespoons reduced-calorie margarine
¼ cup finely chopped onion
3 cloves garlic, minced
8 ounces fresh asparagus, peeled and
   sliced diagonally into ½-inch pieces
2 tablespoons dry white wine
2 tablespoons fresh lemon juice
   Freshly ground black pepper
¼ cup (1 ounce) SARGENTO® Grated
   Parmesan Cheese
¾ cup (3 ounces) SARGENTO® Light
   Fancy Shredded Mozzarella Cheese

Chop and measure all ingredients before beginning.
Bring water to a boil. Add pasta; cook to al dente (firm
to the bite). Drain; place in large bowl. Meanwhile,
melt margarine over medium heat in large skillet. Add
onion and garlic; cook and stir until tender. Add
asparagus; cook and stir 2 minutes. Add wine and
lemon juice; simmer 1 minute. Season with pepper to
taste. Remove from heat. Add to hot pasta in large bowl
and add Parmesan cheese; toss lightly to coat. Remove
to serving platter; top with mozzarella cheese. Garnish
with strips of lemon zest, if desired. Serve immediately.

Makes 4 servings

Penne Primavera with Sundried Tomato Sauce

4 cups assorted cut-up vegetables (zucchini, eggplant, peppers, mushrooms)
½ cup GREY POUPON® Dijon Mustard, divided
1 tablespoon olive oil
1 (7-ounce) jar sundried tomato strips in oil, drained
1 clove garlic, minced
2 cups light cream or half-and-half
1 tablespoon chopped fresh basil leaves
1 pound penne pasta, cooked
Grated Parmesan cheese, optional

In large bowl, combine vegetables, 2 tablespoons mustard and oil. Place vegetables on broiler pan; broil for 8 to 10 minutes or until golden and tender, stirring occasionally.

In medium saucepan, over medium heat, sauté sundried tomato strips and garlic for 2 minutes. Reduce heat to low and stir in light cream or half-and-half, remaining mustard and basil; heat through.*

In large serving bowl, combine hot cooked pasta, vegetables and cream sauce, tossing to coat well. Serve immediately with Parmesan cheese and garnish, if desired.   *Makes 6 servings*

*If sauce thickens upon standing before tossing with pasta, thin with additional light cream or half-and-half.

Tortellini Primavera

1   cup sliced mushrooms
½   cup chopped onion
1   clove garlic, minced
2   tablespoons butter or margarine
1   package (10 ounces) BIRDS EYE®
     Chopped Spinach, thawed, well
     drained
1   container (8 ounces) PHILADELPHIA
     BRAND® Soft Cream Cheese
1   medium tomato, chopped
¼   cup milk
¼   cup (1 ounce) KRAFT® 100% Grated
     Parmesan Cheese
1   teaspoon Italian seasoning
¼   teaspoon salt
¼   teaspoon pepper
8   to 9 ounces fresh or frozen cheese-
     filled tortellini, cooked and drained

Cook and stir mushrooms, onion and garlic in butter
in large skillet. Add remaining ingredients except
tortellini; mix well. Cook until mixture just begins to
boil, stirring occasionally. Stir in tortellini; cook until
thoroughly heated.   *Makes 4 servings*

Pasta Primavera with Ricotta and Herbs

6 ounces uncooked fettuccine
1 cup reduced fat ricotta cheese
½ cup 1% low fat milk
4 teaspoons olive oil
1 clove garlic, minced
½ teaspoon crushed red pepper flakes
1½ cups sliced yellow squash
1½ cups sliced zucchini
1 cup red bell pepper strips
1 cup fresh or frozen peas
1 teaspoon salt free Italian herb blend
½ cup freshly grated Parmesan cheese

1. Cook fettuccine according to package directions, omitting salt. Drain; keep warm. Whisk together ricotta and milk in small bowl.

2. Heat olive oil in large nonstick skillet over medium heat until hot. Add garlic and red pepper flakes. Cook and stir 1 minute. Add yellow squash, zucchini, bell pepper, peas and herb blend. Cook and stir 5 minutes or until vegetables are crisp-tender.

3. Combine fettuccine, vegetables and ricotta cheese mixture in large bowl. Toss to coat evenly. Sprinkle with Parmesan cheese. *Makes 4 servings*

Garlic Parmesan Pasta

⅓ cup butter or margarine
2 teaspoons dried basil, crushed
2 teaspoons lemon juice
1¼ teaspoons LAWRY'S® Garlic Powder
     with Parsley
¾ teaspoon LAWRY'S® Seasoned Salt
8 ounces fettuccine noodles, cooked,
     drained and kept hot
1½ cups broccoli florets, cooked
     crisp-tender
3 tablespoons chopped walnuts
½ cup grated Parmesan or Romano cheese

In large skillet, melt butter with basil, lemon juice,
Garlic Powder with Parsley and Seasoned Salt. Add hot
fettuccine, broccoli and walnuts; toss lightly to coat.
Add cheese; toss to coat.   *Makes 4 servings*

Mostaccioli with Spinach and Feta

    8   ounces mostaccioli or penne
    2   tablespoons olive oil
    1   clove garlic, minced
    3   cups chopped tomatoes
    1   package (10 ounces) fresh spinach,
          stems removed
    ½   cup chopped green onions
    1   package (8 ounces) ATHENOS® Feta
          Cheese with Basil & Tomato,
          crumbled

COOK pasta as directed on package; drain.

HEAT oil in same pot. Cook and stir garlic, tomatoes,
spinach and onions 2 minutes or until spinach is
wilted and mixture is thoroughly heated.

ADD pasta and feta cheese; cook 1 minute.

Makes 6 servings

Tomato Basil Linguine Modena Style

- 1 package PASTA LABELLA® Tomato Basil Linguine
- ¼ cup extra virgin olive oil
- ½ cup julienned red onion
- ½ cup julienned yellow bell pepper
- ½ cup julienned eggplant
- ½ cup julienned zucchini
- ¼ cup chopped fresh basil
- 1 teaspoon dry oregano
- ½ teaspoon garlic powder
- ½ teaspoon onion powder
- ¼ teaspoon salt
- ¼ teaspoon black pepper
- ¼ cup balsamic vinegar
- ⅓ cup chicken broth
- 1½ tablespoons butter
- ¼ cup shredded Parmesan cheese

Cook pasta according to package directions. Meanwhile heat olive oil in large pot over medium heat. Add all vegetables and spices to olive oil. Stir and sauté for 7 minutes. Add balsamic vinegar and chicken broth and simmer for 3 minutes. Next mix in butter and hot al dente pasta; toss well. To finish, portion pasta into bowls, top with shredded Parmesan cheese, and serve.

Serves 3 dinner portions,
4 lunch portions,
6 appetizer portions or
8 side-dish portions

 **Luscious**

LASAGNAS

Vegetable Lasagna

2 cups low fat cottage cheese
   (1% milkfat)
1 (10-ounce) package frozen chopped
   spinach, thawed and well drained
1 cup shredded carrots
½ cup EGG BEATERS® Healthy Real Egg
   Product
2 tablespoons minced onion
1 teaspoon dried Italian seasoning
2 cups no-salt-added spaghetti sauce,
   divided
9 lasagna noodles, cooked in unsalted
   water and drained
1 cup (4 ounces) shredded part-skim
   mozzarella cheese
2 tablespoons grated Parmesan cheese

In medium bowl, combine cottage cheese, spinach,
carrots, Egg Beaters®, onion and Italian seasoning; set
aside.

Spread ½ cup spaghetti sauce on bottom of greased
13×9×2-inch baking dish. Top with 3 noodles and
⅓ *each* spinach mixture and remaining sauce. Repeat
layers 2 more times. Sprinkle with mozzarella and
Parmesan cheeses; cover. Bake at 375°F for 20
minutes. Uncover; bake for 25 minutes more or until
set. Let stand 10 minutes before serving.

Makes 8 servings

Contadina® Classic Lasagna

8 ounces dried lasagna noodles, cooked, drained
1½ pounds lean ground beef
1 cup (1 small) chopped onion
½ cup chopped green bell pepper
1¾ cups (14.5-ounce can) CONTADINA® Dalla Casa Buitoni Recipe Ready Diced Tomatoes, undrained
1 cup (8-ounce can) CONTADINA® Dalla Casa Buitoni Tomato Sauce
⅔ cup (6-ounce can) CONTADINA® Dalla Casa Buitoni Italian Paste with Roasted Garlic
½ cup dry red wine or beef broth
1 tablespoon Italian herb seasoning
1½ teaspoons salt
½ teaspoon ground black pepper
2 cups (8 ounces) shredded mozzarella cheese
1 cup (8 ounces) ricotta cheese
1 egg

CRUMBLE ground beef into large skillet. Add onion and bell pepper. Cook over medium-high heat for 5 to 6 minutes or until beef is no longer pink; drain.

ADD tomatoes and juice, tomato sauce, tomato paste, wine, Italian herb seasoning, salt and pepper; bring to a boil. Reduce heat to low; cook, stirring occasionally, for 20 minutes or until flavors are blended.

COMBINE *1 cup* mozzarella cheese, ricotta cheese and egg in medium bowl. Layer one third of noodles, half of meat sauce, one third of noodles, ricotta cheese mixture, remaining noodles and remaining meat sauce in 13×9-inch baking dish. Sprinkle with *remaining* mozzarella cheese.

BAKE, covered, in preheated 350°F. oven for 45 minutes. Uncover; bake for additional 10 minutes or until cheese is bubbly.   *Makes 10 servings*

Lazy Lasagna

1 **pound ground beef**
1 **jar (32 ounces) spaghetti sauce**
1 **pound cottage cheese**
8 **ounces sour cream**
8 **uncooked lasagna noodles**
3 **packages (6 ounces each) sliced**
    mozzarella cheese (12 slices)
½ **cup grated Parmesan cheese**
1 **cup water**

Cook beef in large skillet over medium-high heat until meat is brown, stirring to separate meat; drain. Add spaghetti sauce. Reduce heat to low. Heat through, stirring occasionally; set aside.

Preheat oven to 350°F. Combine cottage cheese with sour cream in medium bowl; blend well. Spoon 1½ cups of meat sauce onto bottom of 13×9-inch baking pan. Place 4 uncooked noodles over sauce, then half the cottage cheese mixture, 4 slices of mozzarella cheese, half the remaining meat sauce and ¼ cup of Parmesan cheese. Repeat layers starting with the uncooked noodles. Top with remaining slices of mozzarella cheese. Pour water around the sides of the pan. Cover tightly with foil.

Bake 1 hour. Uncover; bake 20 minutes more or until bubbly. Let stand 15 to 20 minutes before cutting.

Makes 8 to 10 servings

Tomato Pesto Lasagna

8 ounces uncooked lasagna noodles
1 pound sausage or ground beef
1 can (14½ ounces) DEL MONTE®
   FreshCut™ Diced Tomatoes with
   Garlic & Onion, undrained
1 can (6 ounces) DEL MONTE® Tomato
   Paste
¾ cup water
8 ounces ricotta cheese
1 package (4 ounces) frozen pesto,
   thawed
8 ounces (2 cups) shredded mozzarella
   cheese

1. Cook noodles according to package directions; rinse, drain and separate noodles.

2. Brown meat in 10-inch skillet; drain. Stir in tomatoes with juice, tomato paste and water; mix well.

3. Layer ⅓ meat sauce, half *each* of noodles, ricotta cheese, pesto and mozzarella cheese in 2-quart or 9-inch square baking dish; repeat layers ending with meat sauce.

4. Bake at 350°F for 30 minutes or until heated through.   *Makes 6 servings*

Microwave Directions: Prepare lasagna noodles as directed above. In 9-inch square microwavable dish, assemble lasagna as directed above. Cover with plastic wrap; cook on HIGH 10 minutes, rotating dish after 5 minutes.

Southwestern Beef and Bean Lasagna

½ pound extra lean ground beef
1 can (16 ounces) pinto beans, drained
1 teaspoon cumin seeds *or* ½ teaspoon
      ground cumin
1 teaspoon olive oil
1½ cups chopped onions
1 tablespoon seeded and minced jalapeño
      pepper
1 clove garlic, minced
4 cups no-salt-added tomato sauce
1 can (4 ounces) diced green chilies,
      undrained
2 teaspoons chili powder
1 teaspoon dried oregano leaves
1 container (8 ounces) nonfat cottage
      cheese
1½ cups (6 ounces) shredded reduced fat
      Cheddar cheese, divided
1 egg white
¼ cup chopped fresh cilantro
½ teaspoon salt
¼ teaspoon black pepper
8 ounces uncooked lasagna noodles
1 cup water

1. Brown beef in large skillet. Drain off fat. Stir in beans; set aside. Place cumin seeds in large nonstick skillet. Cook and stir over medium heat 2 minutes or until fragrant (omit step if using ground cumin). Remove from skillet. In same skillet, heat oil. Add onions, jalapeño and garlic; cook until onions are soft.

Add tomato sauce, green chilies, chili powder, oregano and roasted cumin seeds or ground cumin. Bring to a boil; reduce heat. Simmer, uncovered, 20 minutes.

2. Preheat oven to 350°F. Combine cottage cheese, ½ cup Cheddar cheese, egg white, cilantro, salt and black pepper in medium bowl. Spray 13×9-inch baking pan with nonstick cooking spray. Cover bottom with ¾ cup tomato sauce mixture. Place layer of noodles on sauce. Spread half the beef mixture over noodles, then place another layer of noodles on top. Spread cheese mixture over noodles. Spread with remaining beef mixture. Layer with noodles. Pour remaining sauce mixture over all; sprinkle with remaining 1 cup Cheddar cheese. Pour water around edges. Cover tightly with foil. Bake 1 hour and 15 minutes or until pasta is tender. Cool 10 minutes before serving.

Makes 6 to 10 servings

Italian Sausage Lasagna

1½ pounds BOB EVANS FARMS® Italian
      Roll Sausage
2   tablespoons olive oil
2   green bell peppers, thinly sliced
1   large yellow onion, thinly sliced
4   cloves garlic, minced and divided
1   (28-ounce) can whole tomatoes,
      undrained
1   (8-ounce) can tomato sauce
2   teaspoons fennel seeds
      Salt and black pepper to taste
1   tablespoon butter or margarine
1   large yellow onion, chopped
2   (10-ounce) packages chopped frozen
      spinach, thawed and squeezed dry
1   cup grated Parmesan cheese, divided
3   cups (24 ounces) low fat ricotta cheese
1   pound shredded mozzarella or
      provolone cheese
9   uncooked lasagna noodles

Crumble sausage in large heavy skillet. Cook over
medium heat until well browned, stirring occasionally.
Remove sausage to paper towels; set aside. Drain off
drippings and wipe skillet clean with paper towels.
Heat oil in same skillet over medium-high heat until
hot. Add green peppers, sliced onion and half the
garlic. Cook, covered, over medium heat about 10
minutes or until vegetables are wilted, stirring
occasionally. Stir in tomatoes with juice, tomato sauce
and fennel seeds, stirring well to break up tomatoes.

Bring to a boil. Reduce heat to low; simmer,
uncovered, 20 to 30 minutes to blend flavors. Stir in
reserved sausage.

Season sauce mixture with salt and black pepper; set
aside. Melt butter in small saucepan over medium-high
heat; add chopped onion and remaining garlic. Cook
and stir about 10 minutes or until onion is tender. Stir
in spinach and ¼ cup Parmesan; set aside. Combine
ricotta, mozzarella and ½ cup Parmesan in medium
bowl. Season with salt and black pepper. Cook noodles
according to package directions; drain.

Preheat oven to 350°F. Pour ⅓ of reserved sauce
mixture into greased 13×9-inch baking dish; spread
evenly. Arrange 3 noodles over sauce mixture; spread
half the spinach mixture over noodles. Spread half the
cheese mixture evenly over spinach. Repeat layers
once. Top with remaining 3 noodles and sauce mixture.
Sprinkle with remaining ¼ cup Parmesan. Bake about
1 hour or until sauce is bubbly and cheese is browned
on top. Let stand 10 to 15 minutes before slicing. Serve
hot. Refrigerate leftovers.   *Makes 8 servings*

Lasagne Roll-Ups

8   dried lasagne noodles, cooked, drained and kept warm
1   pound Italian sausage
1   cup (1 small) chopped onion
2   cups (*three* 6-ounce cans) CONTADINA® Dalla Casa Buitoni Italian Paste with Roasted Garlic
2   cups water
1   teaspoon dried oregano, crushed
½   teaspoon dried basil, crushed
1¾   cups (15-ounce container) ricotta cheese
1   package (10 ounces) frozen chopped spinach, thawed, squeezed dry
1½   cups (6 ounces) shredded mozzarella cheese, *divided*
1   cup (4 ounces) grated Parmesan cheese
1   egg
½   teaspoon salt
¼   teaspoon ground black pepper

CRUMBLE sausage into large skillet; add onion. Cook over medium-high heat for 4 to 5 minutes or until sausage is no longer pink; drain. Stir in tomato paste, water, oregano and basil; bring to a boil. Reduce heat to low; cook, covered, for 20 minutes.

COMBINE ricotta cheese, spinach, *1 cup* mozzarella cheese, Parmesan cheese, egg, salt and pepper in large bowl. Spread about ½ cup cheese mixture onto each noodle; roll up. Place, seam-side down, in 13×9-inch baking dish. Pour sauce over rolls. Sprinkle with *remaining* mozzarella cheese.

BAKE, covered, in preheated 350°F. oven for 30 to 40 minutes or until heated through and cheese is melted.

Makes 8 servings

Note: Lasagne Roll-Ups may be prepared ahead of time, covered and refrigerated for several hours or overnight. Allow for additional baking time when refrigerated.

Lasagna Beef 'n' Spinach Roll-Ups

1½ pounds ground beef
 1 (28-ounce) jar spaghetti sauce
 ½ cup A.1.® ORIGINAL or A.1.® BOLD
      Steak Sauce
 ½ teaspoon dried basil leaves
 1 (15-ounce) container ricotta cheese
 1 (10-ounce) package frozen chopped
      spinach, thawed, well drained
 2 cups shredded mozzarella cheese
      (8 ounces)
 ⅓ cup grated Parmesan cheese, divided
 1 egg, beaten
12 lasagna noodles, cooked, drained
 2 tablespoons chopped fresh parsley

In large skillet, over medium-high heat, brown beef until no longer pink, stirring occasionally to break up beef; drain. In small bowl, mix spaghetti sauce, steak sauce and basil; stir 1 cup spaghetti sauce mixture into beef. Set aside remaining sauce mixture.

In medium bowl, mix ricotta cheese, spinach, mozzarella cheese, 3 tablespoons Parmesan cheese and egg. On each lasagna noodle, spread about ¼ cup ricotta mixture. Top with about ⅓ cup beef mixture. Roll up each noodle from short end; lay each roll, seam side down, in lightly greased 13×9×2-inch baking dish. Pour reserved spaghetti sauce mixture over noodles. Sprinkle with remaining Parmesan cheese and parsley. Bake, covered, at 350°F 30 minutes. Uncover and bake 15 to 20 minutes more or until hot and bubbly. Serve with additional Parmesan cheese, if desired. Garnish as desired.   *Makes 6 servings*

Country-Style Lasagna

9   lasagna noodles (2 inches wide)
2   cans (14½ ounces each) DEL MONTE®
     FreshCut™ Diced Tomatoes with
     Garlic & Onion
     Milk
2   tablespoons butter or margarine
3   tablespoons all-purpose flour
1   teaspoon dried basil, crushed
1   cup diced cooked ham
2   cups shredded mozzarella cheese

1. Cook noodles according to package directions; rinse, drain and separate noodles.

2. Drain tomatoes, reserving liquid; pour liquid into measuring cup. Add milk to measure 2 cups. Melt butter in large saucepan; stir in flour and basil. Cook over medium heat 3 minutes, stirring constantly. Stir in reserved liquid; cook until thickened, stirring constantly. Season to taste with salt and pepper, if desired. Stir in tomatoes.

3. Spread thin layer of sauce on bottom of 11×7-inch or 2-quart baking dish. Top with 3 noodles and ⅓ *each* of sauce, ham and cheese; repeat layers twice, ending with cheese. Bake, uncovered, at 375°F, 25 minutes. Garnish with Parmesan cheese or green onions, if desired.   *Makes 6 servings*

Spam™ Lasagna

6 uncooked lasagna noodles
2½ cups chunky spaghetti sauce, divided
2 teaspoons dried basil leaves
1 (12-ounce) can SPAM® Luncheon Meat,
 thinly sliced, divided
2 cups (8 ounces) shredded mozzarella
 cheese, divided
⅓ cup grated Parmesan cheese

Heat oven to 350°F. Cook lasagna noodles according to package directions. In large bowl, combine spaghetti sauce and basil. In 9-inch square baking pan, spread ½ cup spaghetti sauce. Top with 3 lasagna noodles, cutting and overlapping noodles to fit, ½ of the Spam® and ½ of the mozzarella cheese. Spread 1½ cups spaghetti sauce over mozzarella cheese. Repeat layers, ending with spaghetti sauce. Top with Parmesan cheese. Bake 45 to 50 minutes or until thoroughly heated. *Makes 6 servings*

Mexican Lasagna

4 boneless skinless chicken breast halves
2 tablespoons vegetable oil
2 teaspoons chili powder
1 teaspoon ground cumin
1 can (14½ ounces) diced tomatoes with
     garlic, drained
1 can (8 ounces) tomato sauce
1 teaspoon hot pepper sauce (optional)
1 cup part-skim ricotta cheese
1 can (4 ounces) diced green chilies
¼ cup chopped fresh cilantro, divided
12 (6-inch) corn tortillas
1 cup (4 ounces) shredded Cheddar
     cheese

PREHEAT oven to 375°F.

CUT chicken into ½-inch pieces. Heat oil in large skillet over medium heat until hot. Add chicken, chili powder and cumin. Cook about 4 minutes or until browned, stirring occasionally. Stir in tomatoes, tomato sauce and hot pepper sauce, if desired; bring to a boil. Reduce heat; simmer 2 minutes.

COMBINE ricotta cheese, chilies and 2 tablespoons cilantro in small bowl; mix until well blended.

SPOON half of chicken mixture onto bottom of 12×8-inch baking dish. Top with 6 tortillas, ricotta cheese mixture, remaining tortillas, remaining chicken mixture, Cheddar cheese and remaining cilantro. Bake 25 minutes or until heated through.

Makes 6 to 8 servings

Chicken and Veggie Lasagna

Tomato-Herb Sauce (page 291)
Nonstick olive oil cooking spray
1½ cups thinly sliced zucchini
1 cup thinly sliced carrots
3 cups torn fresh spinach leaves
½ teaspoon salt
1 package (15 ounces) fat free ricotta
cheese
½ cup grated Parmesan cheese
9 lasagna noodles, cooked, drained
2 cups (8 ounces) reduced-fat shredded
mozzarella cheese

1. Prepare Tomato-Herb Sauce.

2. Preheat oven to 350°F. Spray large nonstick skillet with cooking spray; heat over medium heat until hot. Add zucchini and carrots; cook and stir about 5 minutes or until almost tender. Remove from heat; stir in spinach and salt.

3. Combine ricotta and Parmesan cheese in small bowl. Spread 1⅔ cups Tomato-Herb Sauce on bottom of 13×9-inch baking pan. Top with 3 noodles. Spoon half the ricotta cheese mixture over noodles; spread lightly with spatula. Spoon half the zucchini mixture over ricotta cheese mixture; sprinkle with 1 cup mozzarella cheese. Repeat layers; place remaining 3 noodles on top.

4. Spread remaining Tomato-Herb Sauce over noodles. Cover with aluminum foil; bake 1 hour or until sauce is bubbly. Let stand 5 to 10 minutes; cut into rectangles. Garnish as desired. *Makes 12 servings*

Tomato-Herb Sauce

Nonstick olive oil cooking spray
- 1½ cups chopped onions (about 2 medium)
- 4 cloves garlic, minced
- 1 tablespoon dried basil leaves
- 1 teaspoon dried oregano leaves
- ½ teaspoon dried tarragon leaves
- ¼ teaspoon dried thyme leaves
- 2½ pounds ripe tomatoes, peeled, cut into wedges
- 1 pound ground chicken, cooked, crumbled, drained
- ¾ cup water
- ¼ cup no-salt-added tomato paste
- ½ teaspoon salt
- ½ teaspoon pepper

1. Spray large nonstick skillet with cooking spray; heat over medium heat until hot. Add onions, garlic, basil, oregano, tarragon and thyme; cook and stir about 5 minutes or until onions are tender.

2. Add tomatoes, chicken, water and tomato paste; heat to a boil. Reduce heat to low and simmer, uncovered, about 20 minutes or until sauce is reduced to 5 cups. Stir in salt and pepper.   *Makes 5 cups*

Turkey Lasagna

1 pound Italian turkey sausage
1 jar (25.5 ounces) reduced-calorie
    vegetable spaghetti sauce
2 cups non-fat cottage cheese
1 cup shredded low-fat mozzarella cheese
¼ cup plus 2 tablespoons grated
    Parmesan cheese, divided
    Vegetable cooking spray
8 uncooked lasagna noodles

1. Crumble sausage into large nonstick skillet. Sauté over medium-high heat 9 minutes or until no longer pink. Drain. Stir in sauce.

2. In medium bowl, combine cottage cheese, mozzarella cheese and ¼ cup Parmesan cheese.

3. Spray 13×9-inch baking pan with cooking spray. Spread 1 cup meat sauce onto bottom of prepared pan. Place 4 uncooked noodles over sauce, breaking to fit if necessary. Spread ½ of cheese mixture over noodles. Layer with ½ of remaining sauce, 4 noodles and remaining cheese mixture. Top with remaining sauce, covering all noodles. Sprinkle with 2 tablespoons Parmesan cheese. Cover pan tightly with aluminum foil. Bake at 350°F for 45 minutes or until noodles are tender. Let stand 10 to 15 minutes before cutting to serve.   *Makes 8 servings*

Favorite recipe from **National Turkey Federation**

Broccoli Lasagna Bianca

1 (15- to 16-ounce) container fat-free
   ricotta cheese
1 cup EGG BEATERS® Healthy Real Egg
   Product
1 tablespoon minced basil *or* 1 teaspoon
   dried basil leaves
½ cup chopped onion
1 clove garlic, minced
2 tablespoons margarine
¼ cup all-purpose flour
2 cups skim milk
2 (10-ounce) packages frozen chopped
   broccoli, thawed and well drained
1 cup (4 ounces) shredded part-skim
   mozzarella cheese
9 lasagna noodles, cooked and drained
1 small tomato, chopped
2 tablespoons grated Parmesan cheese
   Fresh basil leaves for garnish

In medium bowl, combine ricotta cheese, Egg Beaters®
and minced basil; set aside. In large saucepan, over
medium heat, sauté onion and garlic in margarine
until tender-crisp. Stir in flour; cook for 1 minute.
Gradually stir in milk; cook, stirring until mixture
thickens and begins to boil. Remove from heat; stir in
broccoli and mozzarella cheese.

In lightly greased 13×9×2-inch baking dish, place 3
lasagna noodles; top with ⅓ *each* ricotta and broccoli
mixtures. Repeat layers 2 more times. Top with tomato;
sprinkle with Parmesan cheese. Bake at 350°F for 1
hour or until set. Let stand 10 minutes before serving.
Garnish with basil leaves.   *Makes 8 servings*

Seafood Lasagna with Spaghetti Squash and Broccoli

 1 tablespoon olive oil
 1 cup minced shallots
16 small mushrooms, cut in half
 1 tablespoon minced garlic (2 to 4 cloves)
 1 teaspoon dried thyme leaves
 3 tablespoons all-purpose flour
 2 cups dry white wine or chicken broth
 1 cup bottled clam juice
 ¼ teaspoon freshly ground nutmeg
   Ground pepper to taste
1½ pounds cooked seafood mixture of
      firm-textured fish (such as salmon)
      and scallops, cut into bite-size pieces,
      divided
 6 lasagna noodles, cooked and drained
 4 ounces (1½ to 2 cups) stuffing mix
 1 (10-ounce) package frozen chopped
      broccoli, thawed
 1 pound JARLSBERG LITE™ Cheese,
      shredded
 3 cups cooked spaghetti squash

Heat oil in large skillet over medium-high heat. Sauté shallots, mushrooms, garlic and thyme in oil 4 minutes or until shallots begin to brown. Add flour; cook, stirring constantly, 2 to 3 minutes. Add wine, clam juice, nutmeg and pepper. Boil 3 minutes to thicken and reduce liquid. Add fish pieces and simmer 3 minutes. Add scallops; remove skillet from heat and set aside.

Arrange 3 lasagna noodles on bottom of 3½-quart, rectangular baking dish. Evenly sprinkle with stuffing mix. Reserve 1 cup sauce mixture; spoon remaining sauce mixture over stuffing mix. Cover evenly with broccoli, ⅔ of cheese and 2 cups spaghetti squash. Cover with remaining lasagna noodles, cheese, reserved sauce mixture and remaining spaghetti squash. Press down firmly.* Cover tightly with tented foil and bake at 350°F for 45 to 50 minutes or until heated through.   *Makes 10 to 12 servings*

*Recipe can be made ahead up to this point and refrigerated. Bring to room temperature before baking.

Tip: To cook spaghetti squash, pierce in several places and place on baking sheet in 350°F oven for 1 hour or until tender when pierced with knife. When squash is cool, cut in half, scoop out seeds and remove strands with two forks. Squash may be prepared ahead and refrigerated until needed.

Lasagne Rolls

2 tablespoons olive oil, divided
4 ounces cremini or white mushrooms, chopped
½ cup chopped onion
2 garlic cloves, minced
1 package (about 1¼ pounds) PERDUE®
    Fresh Ground Chicken, Ground
    Turkey or Ground Turkey Breast
    Meat
2 tablespoons butter or margarine
¼ cup all-purpose flour
1¼ cups milk
    Salt and ground pepper to taste
    Dash grated nutmeg
16 curly lasagne noodles, cooked
    al dente
2 packages (10 ounces each) frozen
    chopped spinach, thawed and well
    drained
¼ cup shredded mozzarella cheese
2 cups marinara sauce

Preheat oven to 350°F. Grease large shallow baking dish. In large skillet over medium-high heat, heat 1 tablespoon oil. Add mushrooms, onion and garlic; sauté 2 to 3 minutes. Add chicken; sauté 5 minutes or until cooked through. With slotted spoon, remove chicken mixture from skillet. Add butter to remaining liquid in skillet; melt over medium-high heat. Add flour and whisk to blend; cook 2 to 3 minutes, whisking often. Whisk in milk until thickened (sauce will be very thick). Return chicken mixture to skillet and stir well. Season with salt, pepper and nutmeg. Lay lasagne noodles on work surface. Divide spinach among noodles and spread out in a thin layer. Divide chicken mixture among noodles and spread out in a thin layer. Sprinkle noodles with mozzarella. Roll noodles up, jelly-roll style, enclosing filling; place in prepared baking dish, curly side down. Spoon marinara sauce over and around rolls. Bake, loosely covered, 20 to 30 minutes until hot and bubbly.

Makes 8 servings

Fresh Vegetable Lasagna

- 8 ounces uncooked lasagna noodles
- 1 package (10 ounces) frozen chopped spinach, thawed, well drained
- 1 cup shredded carrots
- ½ cup sliced green onions
- ½ cup sliced red bell pepper
- ¼ cup chopped fresh parsley
- ½ teaspoon ground black pepper
- 1½ cups low fat cottage cheese
- 1 cup buttermilk
- ½ cup plain nonfat yogurt
- 2 egg whites
- 1 cup sliced mushrooms
- 1 can (14 ounces) artichoke hearts, drained and chopped
- 2 cups (8 ounces) shredded part-skim mozzarella cheese
- ¼ cup freshly grated Parmesan cheese

1. Cook pasta according to package directions, omitting salt. Drain. Rinse under cold water; drain well. Set aside.

2. Preheat oven to 375°F. Pat spinach with paper towels to remove excess moisture. Combine spinach, carrots, green onions, bell pepper, parsley and black pepper in large bowl. Set aside.

3. Combine cottage cheese, buttermilk, yogurt and egg whites in food processor or blender; process until smooth.

4. Spray 13×9-inch baking pan with nonstick cooking spray. Arrange one third of lasagna noodles on bottom of pan. Spread with half *each* of cottage cheese mixture, vegetable mixture, mushrooms, artichokes and mozzarella. Repeat layers, ending with noodles. Sprinkle with Parmesan.

5. Cover and bake 30 minutes. Remove cover; continue baking 20 minutes or until bubbly and heated through. Let stand 10 minutes before serving.

Makes 8 servings

Lasagna Primavera

1 (8-ounce) package lasagna noodles
3 carrots, cut into ¼-inch-thick slices
1 cup broccoli flowerets
1 cup zucchini, cut into ¼-inch-thick slices
1 crookneck squash, cut into ¼-inch-thick slices
2 (10-ounce) packages frozen chopped spinach, thawed
1 (8-ounce) package ricotta cheese
1 (26-ounce) jar NEWMAN'S OWN® Marinara Sauce with Mushrooms
3 cups (12 ounces) shredded mozzarella cheese
½ cup (2 ounces) grated Parmesan cheese

Bring 3 quarts water to a boil in 6-quart saucepan over high heat. Add lasagna noodles and cook 5 minutes. Add carrots; cook 2 more minutes. Add broccoli, zucchini and crookneck squash; cook for 2 minutes or until pasta is tender. Drain well.

Squeeze liquid out of spinach. Combine spinach with ricotta cheese. In a 3-quart rectangular baking pan, spread ⅓ of the Newman's Own® Marinara Sauce with Mushrooms. Line pan with lasagna noodles. Layer ½ *each* of the vegetables, spinach mixture and mozzarella cheese over the noodles; top with ½ of the remaining Newman's Own® Marinara Sauce with Mushrooms. Repeat layers. Sprinkle with Parmesan cheese.

Place baking pan on 15×10-inch baking sheet that has been lined with foil. Bake, uncovered, in a 400°F oven approximately 30 minutes or until hot in the center. Let stand 10 minutes before serving.

Makes 8 servings

Note: Lasagna may be prepared up to 2 days before baking and refrigerated, covered. Remove from refrigerator 1 hour before baking. If cold, bake for 1 hour at 350°F.

Broccoli Lasagna

1 tablespoon CRISCO® Vegetable Oil
1 cup chopped onion
3 cloves garlic, minced
1 can (14½ ounces) tomatoes, undrained
    and chopped
1 can (8 ounces) tomato sauce
1 can (6 ounces) tomato paste
1 cup thinly sliced fresh mushrooms
¼ cup chopped fresh parsley
1 tablespoon red wine vinegar
1 teaspoon dried oregano leaves
1 teaspoon dried basil leaves
1 bay leaf
½ teaspoon salt
¼ teaspoon crushed red pepper
1½ cups lowfat cottage cheese
1 cup (4 ounces) shredded low moisture
    part-skim mozzarella cheese, divided
6 lasagna noodles, cooked and well
    drained
3 cups chopped broccoli, cooked and well
    drained
1 tablespoon grated Parmesan cheese

1. Heat oven to 350°F. Oil 11¾×7½×2-inch baking dish lightly.

2. Heat 1 tablespoon Crisco® Oil in large saucepan on medium heat. Add onion and garlic. Cook and stir until tender. Stir in tomatoes, tomato sauce, tomato paste, mushrooms, parsley, vinegar, oregano, basil, bay leaf, salt and crushed red pepper. Bring to a boil. Reduce heat to low. Cover. Simmer 30 minutes, stirring occasionally. Remove bay leaf.

3. Combine cottage cheese and ½ cup mozzarella cheese in small bowl. Stir well.

4. Place 2 lasagna noodles onto bottom of baking dish. Layer with 1 cup broccoli, ⅓ of tomato sauce and ⅓ of cottage cheese mixture. Repeat layers two times. Cover with foil.

5. Bake at 350°F for 25 minutes. Uncover. Sprinkle with remaining ½ cup mozzarella cheese and Parmesan cheese. Bake, uncovered, 10 minutes or until cheese melts. Let stand 10 minutes before serving.

Makes 8 servings

Three Cheese Vegetable Lasagna

1 large onion, chopped
3 cloves garlic, minced
1 teaspoon olive oil
1 can (28 ounces) no-salt-added tomato purée
1 can (14½ ounces) no-salt-added tomatoes, undrained and chopped
2 cups (6 ounces) sliced fresh mushrooms
1 zucchini, diced
1 large green bell pepper, chopped
2 teaspoons basil, crushed
1 teaspoon *each* salt and sugar (optional)
½ teaspoon *each* red pepper flakes and oregano, crushed
2 cups (15 ounces) SARGENTO® Light Ricotta Cheese
1 package (10 ounces) frozen chopped spinach, thawed and squeezed dry
2 egg whites
2 tablespoons (½ ounce) SARGENTO® Fancy Shredded Parmesan Cheese
½ pound lasagna noodles, cooked according to package directions, without oil or salt
¾ cup (3 ounces) *each* SARGENTO® Light Fancy Shredded Mozzarella and Mild Cheddar Cheese, divided

Spray large skillet with nonstick vegetable spray. Add onion, garlic and olive oil; cook over medium heat until tender, stirring occasionally. Add tomato purée, tomatoes with liquid, mushrooms, zucchini, bell pepper, basil, salt, sugar, pepper flakes and oregano. Heat to a boil. Reduce heat; cover and simmer 10 minutes or until vegetables are crisp-tender.

Combine Ricotta cheese, spinach, egg whites and Parmesan cheese; mix well. Spread 1 cup sauce on bottom of 13×9-inch baking dish. Layer 3 lasagna noodles over sauce. Top with half of Ricotta cheese mixture and 2 cups of remaining sauce. Repeat layering with 3 more lasagna noodles, remaining Ricotta mixture and 2 cups sauce. Combine Mozzarella and Cheddar cheeses. Sprinkle ¾ cup cheese mixture over sauce. Top with remaining lasagna noodles and sauce. Cover with foil; bake at 375°F 30 minutes. Uncover; bake 15 minutes more. Sprinkle with remaining ¾ cup cheese mixture. Let stand 10 minutes before serving. *Makes 10 servings*

Pasta Roll-Ups

1 package (1.5 ounces) LAWRY'S®
   Original Style Spaghetti Sauce Spices
   & Seasonings
1 can (6 ounces) tomato paste
2¼ cups water
2 tablespoons butter or vegetable oil
2 cups cottage cheese or ricotta cheese
1 cup (4 ounces) grated mozzarella
   cheese
¼ cup grated Parmesan cheese
2 eggs, lightly beaten
½ to 1 teaspoon LAWRY'S® Garlic Salt
½ teaspoon dried basil, crushed (optional)
8 ounces lasagna noodles, cooked and
   drained

In medium saucepan, prepare Original Style Spaghetti
Sauce Spices & Seasonings according to package
directions using tomato paste, water and butter. In
large bowl, combine remaining ingredients except
noodles; blend well. Spread ¼ cup cheese mixture on
entire length of each lasagna noodle; roll up.

Place noodles, seam side down, in microwave-safe
baking dish. Cover with vented plastic wrap and
microwave on HIGH 6 to 7 minutes or until cheese
begins to melt. Pour sauce over rolls and microwave on
HIGH 1 minute longer, if necessary, to heat sauce.

Makes 6 servings

The publishers would like to thank the companies and organizations listed below for the use of their recipes and photographs in this publication.

Alpine Lace Brands, Inc.
American Italian Pasta Company
American Lamb Council
Best Foods, a Division of CPC International Inc.
Birds Eye
Blue Diamond Growers
Bob Evans Farms®
California Olive Industry
California Table Grape Commission
Chef Paul Prudhomme's® Magic Seasoning Blends®
Cherry Marketing Institute, Inc.
Del Monte Corporation
Filippo Berio Olive Oil
Golden Grain/Mission Pasta
Guiltless Gourmet, Incorporated
Healthy Choice®
Heinz U.S.A.
Holland House, a division of Cadbury Beverages Inc.
Hormel Foods Corporation
Hunt-Wesson, Inc.
The HVR Company

Kikkoman International Inc.
Kraft Foods, Inc.
Lawry's® Foods, Inc.
McIlhenny Company
Nabisco, Inc.
National Fisheries Institute
National Foods, Inc.
National Pasta Association
National Turkey Federation
Nestlé Food Company
Newman's Own, Inc.®
Norseland, Inc.
North Dakota Beef Commission
North Dakota Wheat Commission
Perdue Farms Incorporated
The Procter & Gamble Company
Reckitt & Colman Inc.
Sargento® Foods Inc.
Sonoma Dried Tomato
StarKist® Seafood Company
Walnut Marketing Board
Washington Apple Commission
Wisconsin Milk Marketing Board

VOLUME MEASUREMENTS (dry)

⅛ teaspoon = 0.5 mL
¼ teaspoon = 1 mL
½ teaspoon = 2 mL
¾ teaspoon = 4 mL
1 teaspoon = 5 mL
1 tablespoon = 15 mL
2 tablespoons = 30 mL
¼ cup = 60 mL
⅓ cup = 75 mL
½ cup = 125 mL
⅔ cup = 150 mL
¾ cup = 175 mL
1 cup = 250 mL
2 cups = 1 pint = 500 mL
3 cups = 750 mL
4 cups = 1 quart = 1 L

VOLUME MEASUREMENTS (fluid)

1 fluid ounce (2 tablespoons) = 30 mL
4 fluid ounces (½ cup) = 125 mL
8 fluid ounces (1 cup) = 250 mL
12 fluid ounces (1½ cups) = 375 mL
16 fluid ounces (2 cups) = 500 mL

WEIGHTS (mass)

½ ounce = 15 g
1 ounce = 30 g
3 ounces = 90 g
4 ounces = 120 g
8 ounces = 225 g
10 ounces = 285 g
12 ounces = 360 g
16 ounces = 1 pound = 450 g

DIMENSIONS

1/16 inch = 2 mm
⅛ inch = 3 mm
¼ inch = 6 mm
½ inch = 1.5 cm
¾ inch = 2 cm
1 inch = 2.5 cm

OVEN TEMPERATURES

250°F = 120°C
275°F = 140°C
300°F = 150°C
325°F = 160°C
350°F = 180°C
375°F = 190°C
400°F = 200°C
425°F = 220°C
450°F = 230°C

BAKING PAN SIZES

Utensil	Size in Inches/Quarts	Metric Volume	Size in Centimeters
Baking or Cake Pan (square or rectangular)	8×8×2	2 L	20×20×5
	9×9×2	2.5 L	23×23×5
	12×8×2	3 L	30×20×5
	13×9×2	3.5 L	33×23×5
Loaf Pan	8×4×3	1.5 L	20×10×7
	9×5×3	2 L	23×13×7
Round Layer Cake Pan	8×1½	1.2 L	20×4
	9×1½	1.5 L	23×4
Pie Plate	8×1¼	750 mL	20×3
	9×1¼	1 L	23×3
Baking Dish or Casserole	1 quart	1 L	—
	1½ quart	1.5 L	—
	2 quart	2 L	—